THE
SALAD
KITCHEN

THE
SALAD
KITCHEN

Courtney Roulston

NEW
HOLLAND

Introduction

I loved cooking from a young age. I was raised the youngest of six, and growing up, we didn't have a lot of money but that didn't mean that we ate poorly. There were always ways and means. We were fortunate to own a brood of chickens and so had a ready supply of eggs, as well as Gerty the trusty cow for our milk, and best of all a productive, vegetable patch for afternoon vegie picking.

Holidays were usually very relaxed. We'd spend them fishing and catching fresh crabs and shrimp. At the time, I was oblivious to the fact that I was very lucky to be brought up learning how to cook fresh food that we'd caught or grown for ourselves.

The fact of the matter was, food was always on the agenda in our house, (and perhaps there was a certain fear of never having enough) and so it came naturally to me to start cooking as a hobby. Also, as I was quite shy back then and had five more boisterous older siblings, I saw it as an opportunity to gain my own bit of attention.

Both my parents worked, so I would often take instruction over the phone from them after school on how to prepare dinner. They'd guide me through how to cook a roast lamb and instructed me on the different timings the vegetables needed. I never burnt the house down, or gave food poisoning to my siblings, so I must have been doing something right.

Aside from the lamb, our meals were fairly standard fare and included foods such as grilled (broiled) chops, roasts and barbeques, all served with plain vegetables. My mother ran a fashion shop with a kitchen out the back and she used to employ ladies to come in and help out with alterations of the clothes. I remember an Italian and a Greek lady helping out at the shop and in no time, they started sharing their recipes with us. From then on, the meals we cooked at home started to change and soon we were making Italian olive oil focaccia breads, fresh pastas, pastries such as baklavas and koulourakias and an array of other Greek dishes that, to this day, I am still unable to pronounce.

So, there was the beginning of my desire to try my hand at cooking foods from all different cultures and backgrounds. Not only that, it also gave me the aspiration to travel all over the world during my teens, and those experiences influence my cooking today.

You may be thinking, but why salads? Well, I love to eat salads. I also love to create salads and I have a real passion for trying to create different, modern, hearty dishes to get people excited. I'm always asked for my recipes too and after years of sending recipes to fellow enthusiasts, I figured I should share them in a book.

The book is divided into nine chapters, including a great little section called, 'Tricks and Tips' where I'll let you in on some of my biggest cooking secrets. The rest of my chapters are arranged according to the main food component for your convenience.

All my dishes are designed for sharing. Let's say you want something really light, in which case I'd recommend a delicious salad sashimi recipe. Or, you might be cooking a dinner party for ten and in this case, I'd recommend you try my mouthwateringly good lamb shoulder salad.

You may also notice that throughout the book I've used lots of herbs, dressings and several different textures. I feel these three components make the salad. The herbs give flavour whilst keeping the salad fresh & healthy, the dressings tie all the ingredients together and ensure all the different elements of the dish are bound together in unity! The textures add substance to the salad. That small handful of friend shallots scattered over the top of your salad not only looks great but it also adds crunch and an element of surprise to your dish.

Feel free to substitute any of the listed ingredients to that which you have on hand, or what's in season. All of the recipes are made from scratch. You'll feel good after eating them, I promise.

So, what are you waiting for? Get in the kitchen, start chopping, be creative and enjoy my salads.

Happy cooking!

Contents

Tricks & Tips

Tricks and Tips

Here are a few hints to help keep your salads interesting as well as to get more out of your vegetables and create less waste.

Base your salads on what is in season: Vegetables and fruit that are in season are at their best for eating, have peak nutritional value and often cost a lot less as there is an abundance of stock. Having a shopping list is good for the those who like to be organised, but why not give shopping for fruit and vegetables a go without using a list? See what looks and smells good, pick a few items that are in season and that you like to eat. This is good for anyone that likes to get creative with ingredients and doesn't mind presenting 'mystery salads' or those made up from what is on hand rather than prescriptively following a recipe. Remember, it's good to try new foods. Also, often the best meals can be made from a few simple, seasonal ingredients creatively put together.

Eat skins, don't peel: A lot of the nutrients that fruit and vegetables contain are in or just beneath the skin. Carrots, potatoes, parsnips, zucchinis (courgettes), pumpkins, peaches, pears, apples and tomatoes don't need peeling. Give them a good wash and they're ready to go.

For vegetables that you do peel, I recommend keeping a zip-lock bag in the freezer to collect all your vegetable peelings and trimmings. These are great to have on hand to make fresh stocks.

Buy leaf to stalk vegetables where possible. Use all of the crop, minimise waste and maximise your thriftiness. Did you know you can eat the green leafy tops of carrots? They are creamy and delicious and can be used blended raw, cooked into soups and stocks, or used as baby herbs to garnish dishes. Try throwing a handful into a green smoothie, or my personal favourite, blitzed into a mind-blowing pesto along with cashews, olive oil and Parmesan, see page 219.

Beetroot is another great example. Try and find bunches with the leaves intact. The baby inner leaves are great tossed through salads or used as garnish. The larger leaves are perfect for wilting in a little olive oil or butter for a few minutes. Serve the leaves warm with some crumbled feta or goat's cheese, a handful of roasted hazelnuts, a squeeze of lemon and you'll never throw the leaves out again.

Try to include legumes, seeds and nuts in your dishes. We often think of ingredients such as beef, chicken, pork or seafood as the source of our protein in salads, but it's great to go meat free and replace the traditional protein element with foods such as chickpeas, quinoa, beans, lentils or even the humble, boiled egg to get a protein-packed salad.

Toasted seeds and nuts are also packed with nutrients and good fats. They add wonderful texture to salads as well as additional flavour. There are plenty to try too, either plain or toasted. Mix them through (or sprinkle on top of) your salad to take it to the next level.

Go crazy with fresh herbs! Fresh herbs have 100 per cent flavour and zero calories. Add whole bunches to your salads to boost flavour, freshness and your intake of greens. Most fresh herbs are best kept wrapped in damp kitchen paper in the refrigerator. Any herbs you may have that are looking tired are perfect for blitzing up with your favourite nuts, Parmesan and olive oil to make pesto. The pesto will keep for 4–5 days in the refrigerator or can be frozen into ice trays and later thawed to be used in your favourite tomato salad, tossed through cooked pasta or swirled through hot soups.

Invest in a toothed vegetable peeler or mandolin: Toothed peelers are great for creating 'noodles' out of vegetables such as carrot, zucchini (courgettes), daikon radish, celeriac and beetroot. Mandolins are great for getting consistent wafer thin slices or matchsticks of fruits and vegetables. Changing the shape and size you cut a vegetable is a great way of getting variety into the textures and look of your salads. We eat with our eyes after all.

Get pickling: Most vegetables can be pickled. If you have overbought or are going away and not sure what to do with all the excess vegetables in the crisper, then why not try pickling them? Pickling preserves the lifespan of fresh vegetables and gives a delicious sweet and sour tang. Cabbage, onions, beetroots, carrots, zucchini (courgettes), cucumber, asparagus, chillies, garlic, celeriac, mushrooms, cauliflower and radishes to name a few are all pickle-friendly vegetables.

Waste not, want not. Do you toss out onion skins, the outer leaves of lettuce, the stalks and roots from herbs or broccoli stems? Well, here are a few clever things you can do with those compost bin-bound beauties:

* Onion skins: They're great for stocks and gravies. And, did you know, if you add them to the boiling water you're about to poach your eggs in, they'll infuse a great savoury flavour and can give a 'marbled' effect? Just crack the shells and leave the eggs to sit in the onion-infused water for a few minutes, and that's precisely what'll happen. Give it a go.
* Outer lettuce leaves: We often peel off the darker and not so sweet outer leaves from lettuce. I say keep them: they are fantastic when cooked. Try sautéing a diced French shallot or onion in a little olive oil and butter for a few minutes. Add a crushed clove of garlic and a few chopped mushrooms and cook until fragrant. Add a pinch of sea salt, a large handful of frozen peas and the chopped outer lettuce leaves. Continue to cook for 3–4 minutes, or until wilted. Finish with a squeeze of lemon juice and serve warm as a side dish. This hardly costs anything and is an absolute winner.
* Herb stems: Herb stems such as those from parsley or the stalks from thyme and rosemary are great to pop into any homemade stock or soup. Fresh coriander stems and roots are perfect for adding to curry or laksa pastes. They can be washed and frozen until you're ready to use them.

Here are 10 fantastic things to do with broccoli stems:

* Use your toothed peeler to cut them into noodles and toss raw through salads.
* Peel and slice lengthways and use as a crudité for dips.
* Slice and pickle in a mixture of salt, vinegar and sugar: perfect to add to sandwiches, burgers and salads.
* Cut into rounds and toss through your favourite stir-fry or fried rice.
* Steam until tender and top with a fried egg, Parmesan, chopped chilli and a drizzle of olive oil.
* Slice into rounds, toss into a beaten egg and dust with corn meal. Deep fry and sprinkle with sea salt and serve as a 'naughty' snack.
* Simmer in chicken stock with potato and cauliflower until tender, then whiz into a smooth soup.
* Slice lengthways and toss in a hot wok with sesame oil, oyster sauce and Sichuan pepper for a spicy Asian side dish
* Peel, finely grate and add to vegetarian burgers and patties.
* Cut into matchsticks and mix into your favourite slaw recipe.

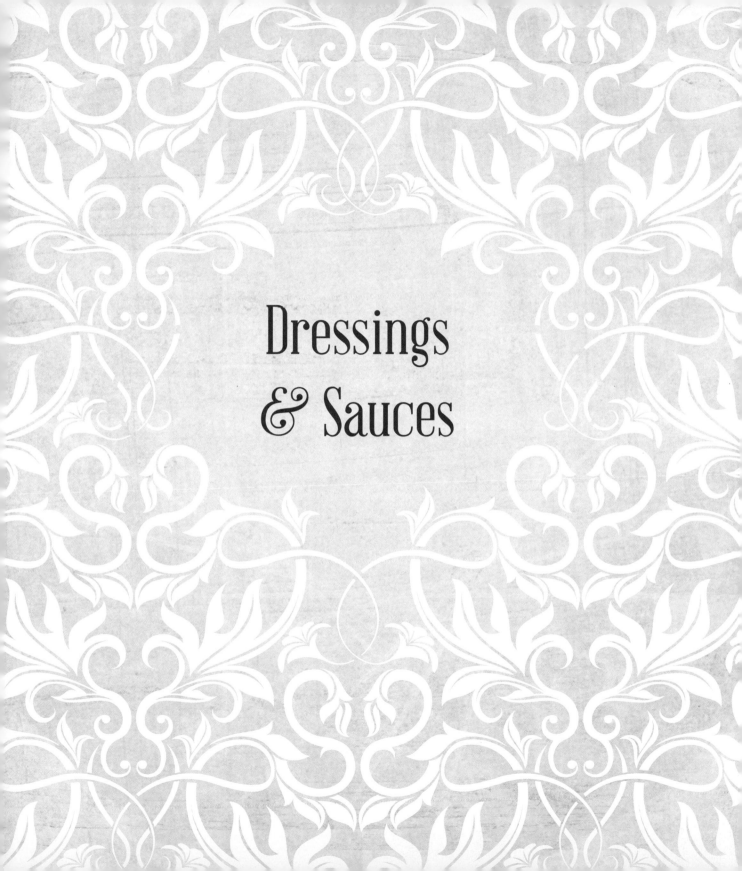

Dressings & Sauces

Tahini Yogurt

Makes about 2 cups/17 fl oz/500 ml

This is one of my favourite dressings to have on hand to 'jazz-up' a multitude of recipes. Roasted carrots spiked with cumin, and served with a generous dollop of tahini yogurt and scattered with fresh coriander (cilantro) is my all time favourite! Try it with any roast or BBQ lamb recipe. Use it on Lebanese flatbread kebabs, roast eggplant (aubergine) salads or a spiced BBQ chicken salad. It'll also work well with chunks of roast pumpkin, caramelised red onion and spicy dukkah salad. I could go on, but if all of that seems too much hard work, it is fabulous just on its own. Eat with raw radish, fennel, carrots and broccoli stalks and used as a dip. Delicious.

Ingredient

1½ cups/12 fl oz/375 ml thick
    Greek (strained plain) yogurt
2 tablespoons white hulled
    tahini paste
1 tablespoon lemon juice
1 tablespoon honey or agave
    syrup
Sea salt flakes and ground
    white pepper

Method

Place the yogurt into a bowl, and using a whisk, mix through the tahini paste until combined. Add in the lemon juice, honey and season with sea salt flakes and a pinch of ground white pepper. Mix through the yogurt and taste for seasoning.

Chopped Egg & Pickle Sauce

Makes about 2 cups/17 fl oz/500 ml

If I was allowed to add pickles to every dish, perhaps I would... I am often caught eating these straight from the jar at home. Pickles add sharpness and a sweet-sour edge to anything they are paired with. This sauce is great with any grilled (broiled) fish, particularly salmon or trout. Try it with shrimp or even your best roast chicken salad!

Ingredient

4 small free-range eggs
½ cup/4 fl oz/125 ml mayonnaise
½ cup/4 fl oz/125 ml Greek (strained plain) yogurt
1 tablespoon lemon juice
1 teaspoon lemon zest
1 teaspoon Dijon mustard
1 teaspoon honey
3 cornichon pickles, finely chopped
1 green spring onion (scallion), finely sliced
¼ cup/2 tablespoons flat leaf parsley, finely chopped
Sea salt flakes and ground white pepper

Method

Bring the eggs to the boil in a pan of salted water and simmer gently for 8–10 minutes. Remove from the heat and using a slotted spoon, place the eggs in a bowl of cold water with a few ice cubes added to stop the eggs cooking further. Leave to cool for 5 minutes before peeling and roughly chopping.

In a large bowl, mix the mayonnaise, yogurt, lemon juice, zest, mustard, honey, pickles, spring onion, parsley and season with a pinch of sea salt flakes and ground white pepper. Mix well to combine and fold through the reserved chopped egg.

Tip

Any of your favourite herbs can be added to this sauce. Why not try chives, dill, capers and tarragon?

Lemon Hummus

Makes around 3 cups/25 fl oz/750 ml

There are many recipes for hummus, and mine is certainly not a traditional one. This takes all of 2 minutes to blitz in a blender, it's inexpensive to make and best of all, it's delicious! This hummus makes a good accompaniment to any spiced lamb recipe. It also pairs well with roast chicken that has been rubbed with Middle Eastern spices and is great eaten as a dip with raw crudité for a healthy afternoon snack.

Ingredients

2 x 14 oz (400 g) cans
chickpeas, drained and
rinsed
2 tablespoons lemon juice
2 tablespoons hulled white
Tahini paste
⅓ cup (2½ fl oz/75 ml) thick
(strained plain) Greek yogurt
1 tablespoon honey
⅓ cup (2½ fl oz/75 ml) olive oil
Sea salt flakes and ground
white pepper

Method

Place all the ingredients into the bowl of a small food processor and season with sea salt flakes and a pinch of ground white pepper. Blend until smooth and creamy. If the mixture looks a little dry while blending, you can add extra olive oil or a small amount of warm water.

Keeps refrigerated for 1 week.

Gochujan Chilli Dressing (Korean Chilli Paste)

Makes around ⅔ cup/5 ½ fl oz/160 ml

Don't be put off by the name of this chilli sauce. It is really easy to make and can be used in lots of different recipes. This sharp and hot sauce is a great condiment to accompany grilled (broiled) meat skewers, stirred through wintery broths and will lift many rice or noodle dishes. Eggs love this chilli sauce, particularly crispy textured fried eggs... and dare I say, it's a good way to shake off a hangover!

Ingredients

- 2 tablespoons sunflower oil or rice bran oil
- 1 large clove garlic, finely grated
- 1 tablespoon fresh ginger, finely grated
- ¼ teaspoon sea salt flakes
- ¼ teaspoon ground white pepper
- 1 tablespoon brown sugar
- 2 tablespoon gochujang (red pepper paste)
- 2 tablespoons rice wine vinegar
- 1 tablespoon light soy sauce

Method

Place the oil into a small pot set over a low heat. Add the garlic and ginger and cook gently for 1–2 minutes, or until fragrant, but not crisp. Remove from the heat and stir in the remaining ingredients until well combined. Taste and season as required, then allow to cool before use.

Keeps refrigerated for 2 weeks.

Notes

Gochujang Korean chilli paste is available in Asian supermarkets

Cheats 'Salad Cream' Dressing

Makes about ½ cup/4 fl oz/125 ml

I created this dressing while away on holiday. With limited ingredients on hand, I managed to whip this up in a flash and let me tell you, it's absolutely delicious! I'd recommend serving this with crispy cos or iceberg lettuce salads, a potato salad or even coleslaw.

Ingredients

⅓ cup (2½ fl oz/75 ml)
   Japanese Kewpie
   mayonnaise
2 teaspoons mild English
   mustard
2 tablespoons lemon juice
1 tablespoon honey
1 tablespoon olive oil
Sea salt flakes and ground
   white pepper

Method

Place all the ingredients into a small bowl and season with a pinch of sea salt and ground white pepper. Whisk until everything is well emulsified before use.

Keeps refrigerated for 1 week.

Za'atar

Makes about ½ cup

This topping is best served sprinkled over roast vegetables or flavoured yogurts. It's also fantastic on Lebanese bread that has been drizzled with olive oil, sprinkled with za'atar and crisped in the oven. Voila.

Most za'atar recipes include store bought dried thyme, which is also fine to use in this recipe. However, sometimes it can have a mustiness so I like to dry my own in the oven for this recipe. It takes no time at all (no pun intended) and the end result is worth the little extra effort.

Ingredients

4 tablespoons fresh thyme leaves, stripped from stems (or equivalent in dried)
2 teaspoons ground sumac
½ teaspoon sea salt flakes
1 tablespoon toasted sesame seeds

Method

Preheat the oven to 160°C/325°F/Gas mark 3. Place the thyme leaves on a lined baking tray and dry in the oven for around 10-15 minutes, or until the leaves crumble when pinched between the fingers. Use a mortar and pestle to finely grind the thyme leaves. Add in the sumac and salt and grind to combine. Stir in the sesame seeds until well combined.

This Za'atar is best used fresh, but will keep for 2 weeks in an airtight container.

Labneh (Yogurt Cheese Balls)

Makes around 15

Labneh is simply unsweetened yogurt, which has been strained to remove its whey. The resulting thick and creamy, soft yogurt cheese can be served on its own, as part of a cheese board, or rolled in fresh herbs or dukkah and stored in jars of olive oil. I love labneh with grilled zucchini (broiled courgettes), lemon, chilli and mint.

Ingredients
1 kg (2¼ lb) thick Greek
  (strained plain) yogurt
1 teaspoon sea salt flakes
1 cup/8 fl oz/250 ml olive oil

Method
Mix the salt into the yogurt. Arrange a 40 cm (16 inch) square of cheesecloth (muslin) on a clean work bench. Place the yogurt into the centre of the cloth, draw up the sides of the cloth and tie a knot with the corners to form a ball. Place a wooden spoon handle through the knot of the cheesecloth and suspend it over a large bowl to catch the liquid as it drains from the yogurt. The liquid is known as the whey. Alternatively, put a sieve over a large bowl and place the cloth and its contents inside the sieve to drain in the refrigerator for 3 days.

Once drained, discard the whey. Using clean hands, roll the yogurt 'cheese' into golf ball-size rounds. Place each on a lined tray and dry out uncovered in the refrigerator for another 3 hours. Place the yogurt balls into a sterilised jar and cover with olive oil.

Labneh will keep for 1 week refrigerated.

Notes
Try spice up labneh by rolling it in different herbs and spices, such as garlic, thyme, oregano, bay leaves, chilli or rosemary, before storing in oil.

Xo Chilli Sauce

Makes around 1½ cups/12 fl oz/375 ml

I first made this chilli sauce when I cooked my signature 'chilli mud crab' dish on MasterChef. This rich and glistening sauce marries perfectly with most seafood... It also works really well with eggs, particularly crispy-fried eggs, mounded with fresh herbs.

Ingredients

¼ cup (2 fl oz/60 ml) sunflower oil

3 golden shallots, finely diced

3 garlic cloves, finely chopped

2 tablespoons fresh ginger, julienned

2 long red chillies, finely chopped

1 tablespoon coriander stems, finely chopped

⅓ cup dried shrimp, soaked in water for 15 minutes, then drained and finely chopped

1 tablespoon caster (superfine) sugar

⅓ cup/2½ fl oz/75 ml shoaxing (Chinese cooking wine)

White pepper

2 teaspoons chilli oil

2 teaspoons sesame oil

1 tablespoon light soy sauce

Method

Heat the sunflower oil in a large frying pan set over medium heat. Add the golden shallots, garlic, ginger, chilli and coriander stems and cook for 3–4 minutes, or until fragrant.

Add the dried shrimp and stir-fry for another 2–3 minutes. Add in the sugar, shoaxing wine, pepper, chilli oil, sesame oil and soy sauce and continue to cook for 5 minutes over a low heat, or until the sauce is a dark, rich red colour and has a shimmer on the surface. Remove from the heat and allow to cool before use.

Leftover sauce will keep for 1 week.

Notes
This sauce can also be used as a stir-fry sauce for crab, chicken, shrimp, eggplant or tofu.

Romesco Sauce

Makes 2 cups/17 fl oz/500 ml

This thick, Spanish sauce is great to use on a variety of recipes. Think of it as a roast capsicum pesto. Grilled chorizo and romesco makes for a great tapas dish but this sauce also works well with grilled (broiled) fish, as a sandwich filler, with roast pumpkin, used as a yummy dip or to garnish a delicious bowl of pumpkin soup.

Ingredients

2 red capsicum (bell pepper),
    quartered and seeds
    removed
2 garlic cloves, unpeeled
1 egg tomato
¼ cup (2 fl oz/60 ml)
    tablespoons extra virgin
    olive oil
3½ oz (100 g) whole roasted
    almonds
1 teaspoon paprika
1 tablespoon red wine vinegar
Sea salt flakes and pepper

Method

Preheat the grill (broiler) on high heat. Place the capsicum, skin-side up, on a lined oven tray with the garlic and whole tomato. Drizzle with 1 tablespoon of the oil and grill (broil), turning occasionally for around 15 minutes, or until the skins have blackened and are slightly blistered. Leave to cool.

Remove and discard the skins from the capsicum, garlic and tomato. Put all three in the bowl of a food processor with the almonds and pulse to a rough paste. Add the remaining oil, paprika and vinegar and blend until combined. Season to taste with sea salt flakes and pepper.

Notes

If you wanted to make a super-quick version of this sauce, you can substitute roast capsicum and semi dried tomatoes from a jar. Try to find jars that contain garlic already.

Basil Pesto

Makes ½ cup/4 fl oz/125ml

For this simple recipe, I've suggested using pine nuts but please feel free to experiment with some of your other favourite nuts. Almonds, macadamia or cashew nuts all work. You'll get a slightly different taste each time.

Ingredients

1 cup firmly packed basil leaves, washed
¼ cup/1 oz/30 g pine nuts
½ garlic clove
30 g Parmesan, freshly grated
⅓ cup/2½ fl oz/75 ml olive oil
2 teaspoons lemon juice
1 teaspoon honey

Method

Place all the ingredients in the bowl of a small food processor. Season with a pinch of ground white pepper and blend until well combined and smooth.

Pesto is best used fresh, but will keep for 5 days in the refrigerator.

Notes

The nuts and herbs in this recipe can be replaced with some of your favourites. Try almonds, macadamias, cashews, parsley, mint or coriander (cilantro).

Herb, Almond & Avocado Chopped Pesto

Makes about 1½ cups/12 fl oz/375 ml

A yummy little twist on the conventional pesto dressing: this sauce is great paired with fresh tomatoes, grilled (broiled) chicken, cold shrimp or poached eggs. It keeps for 2–3 days in the refrigerator.

Ingredients
1 cup loosely packed basil leaves
¼ cup/2 tablespoons mint leaves
¼ cup/2 tablespoons flat leaf parsley
1 green shallot, trimmed
½ garlic clove
⅓ cup/1½ oz/40 g slivered almonds
¾ oz/20 g Parmesan, freshly grated
¼ ripe avocado, peeled
1 tablespoon lemon juice
2 teaspoon honey
⅓ cup/2½ fl oz/75 ml olive oil
Sea salt flakes and ground white pepper

Method
Working on a large wooden chopping board and using a large, sharp knife, roughly chop the basil, mint and parsley. Chop the shallot. Add the garlic, almonds, Parmesan and avocado and continue to chop in a side to side motion until the mixture starts to form a rough paste. Drizzle over the lemon juice, honey and half the oil. Continue to chop the mixture until it has formed a rough green sauce. Place the mixture into a bowl and add the remaining oil and season with sea salt flakes and a pinch of ground white pepper.

Keeps for 2–3 days in the refrigerator.

Fresh Coconut Relish

Makes 1 cup/8 fl oz/250 ml

If you're craving something fresh, light and exotic, try this. It's a great topping for curries, fish dishes, chicken salad or even an Asian-inspired duck salad. Give it a go!

Ingredients

4 tablespoons fresh grated coconut flesh

1 tablespoon lime juice

1 teaspoon caster (superfine) sugar

1 green chilli, seeded and finely chopped

¼ cup/2 tablespoons fresh mint leaves, finely chopped

¼ cup/2 tablespoons coriander (cilantro) leaves, finely chopped

Sea salt flakes

Method

Place the coconut in a bowl along with the lime, sugar, chilli, mint, coriander and a small pinch of salt. Stir well to combine and serve with your favourite salad, or as a sprinkle for curries.

Mustard-Pickled Zucchini

Makes about 3 cups

These pickles work well with all different types of salad ingredients including grilled (broiled) chicken, cured meats, soft cheeses such as ricotta and feta. It's also a great addition to sandwiches: think pastrami and pickles with cheese on rye bread.

Ingredients

- 1 lb 2 oz/500 g small green zucchini (courgettes), thinly sliced
- 1 small white onion, thinly sliced
- 1 tablespoon sea salt flakes
- 2 cups/17 fl oz/500 ml white vinegar
- 1 cup/200 g/7 oz caster (superfine) sugar
- 2 teaspoons ground mustard powder
- 2 teaspoons yellow mustard seeds
- 1 teaspoon ground turmeric

Method

Combine the zucchini, onion, salt and 2 cups (17 fl oz/500 ml) cold water in a non-metallic bowl. Stir to combine and set aside for about 1 hour to soften the zucchini.

Meanwhile, combine the remaining ingredients in a saucepan set over a medium heat. Stir to dissolve the sugar and simmer for 4–5 minutes. Remove from the heat and allow to cool to room temperature.

Drain the zucchini and onion, then return to the bowl. Add the vinegar mixture, stir to combine, then transfer to sterile jars. Top up the jars with water, if needed. Seal and leave to pickle in the refrigerator for 2–3 days before use.

The pickle will keep for at least 2–3 weeks.

Japanese-Style Wafu Dressing

Makes about 1 cup/8 fl oz/250 ml

The onion in this dish adds both mild heat and substance, although if you'd prefer, you can use shallots, red onion or golden shallots... They'll add extra sweetness.

Method

1 small white onion, peeled and roughly chopped

2 tablespoons Japanese soy sauce

2 tablespoons rice wine vinegar

¼ cup/2 fl oz/60 ml sunflower oil

1 tablespoon caster (superfine) sugar

2 teaspoon sesame oil

¼ teaspoon ground white pepper

2 teaspoon toasted sesame seeds

Method

Place all the ingredients except for the sesame seeds in a small food processor or blender. Blend for 1 minute, or until the dressing is smooth. Taste for balance of salty, sweet and sour and adjust, if needed. Add sesame seeds.

Dukkah

Dukkah is one of my favourite 'sprinklers'. You can buy ready made dukkah but nothing compares to the flavours you'll get from toasting your own spices. Scatter it over your favourite salad to add texture and flavour, roll boiled eggs in it, or simply dip some fresh bread and olive oil into it for a little kick.

Ingredients

¼ cup/1 oz/30 g roasted unsalted pistachio kernels
¼ cup/1 oz/30 g roasted unsalted almonds
¼ cup/1 oz/30 g roasted unsalted cashews
1 tablespoon cumin seeds
1 tablespoon coriander seeds
¼ cup/1½ oz/45 g sesame seeds
1 teaspoon fresh ground black pepper
1 teaspoon sea salt flakes

Method

Place the pistachios, almonds and cashews in the bowl of a food processor. Pulse the nuts until coarsely chopped.

Heat the cumin and coriander seeds in a small non-stick frying pan set over a medium heat and toast for 1 minute, or until fragrant. Tip the seeds into a mortar and pestle or a spice grinder, and grind to a powder.

Place the pan back onto the heat and toast the sesame seeds for 2–3 minutes, or until golden. Remove from the heat and place the sesame seeds into a bowl, add the ground spices, chopped nuts and pepper and salt. Stir to combine and place into a sterilised jar.

Dukkah will keep for 2 weeks, but is best used fresh.

Spiced Maple Almonds

Makes 2 cups/8 oz/225 g

This is great treatment to try on any of your favourite nuts. Add a little ground chilli to the mix if you like added heat.

Ingredients
1 egg white
1 tablespoon maple syrup, plus extra to drizzle
2 cups/8 oz/225 g whole almonds
1 teaspoon ground cumin
2 teaspoons mixed (apple pie) spice
½ teaspoon sea salt flakes

Method
Preheat the oven to 170°C/340°F/Gas mark 3½.

Whisk the egg white in a clean, grease-free bowl, until it is light and fluffy. Mix through the maple syrup, almonds, cumin, mixed spice and salt. Stir well to coat then spread the nuts out on a lined baking sheet. Roast for 10 minutes then drizzle with a little extra maple syrup and toss to coat. Roast for another 5–6 minutes, or until the almonds are golden. Remove from the oven and allow to cool before eating.

Breakfast
& Eggs

Bircher Muesli with
Peach & Almond Salad

Serves 6

This recipe is beautiful. You'll love it if you want a healthy, nutritious and hearty start to your day. It's very moreish indeed—probably a good thing. It'll keep for 5 days in your refrigerator. Start this recipe the night before you intend to eat it.

Ingredients

9 oz/250 g rolled oats

7 fl oz/200 ml whole (full fat) milk

3½ fl oz/100 ml apple juice (fresh or cloudy)

3½ fl oz/100 ml orange juice

Juice of 1 lime

2¾ oz/80 g whole almonds, chopped

1¾ oz/50 g honey, plus extra to serve

½ teaspoon ground cinnamon

2½ oz/75 g sultanas (golden raisins)

2 large green eating apples

4½ oz/125 g natural (plain) yogurt

2 large ripe peaches, sliced

1 ripe mango, peeled and sliced

2 passionfruit or seasonal fruits of your choice

Sea salt flakes

Method

Put the oats into a large bowl with the milk, apple juice, orange juice, lime juice, half the almonds, all the honey, cinnamon, sultanas and a pinch of salt. Stir together, and cover with cling film (plastic wrap) and place in the refrigerator.

The next morning, coarsely grate the apples and mix into the soaked oats along with the yogurt. Stir well.

Top the bircher muesli with sliced peach, mango, passion fruit and the remaining almonds. Drizzle with extra honey if you like.

This bircher muesli will keep in the refrigerator for up to 5 days.

Soy & Coconut Chia Pudding with Strawberry & Sesame

Serves 4-6

This chilled pudding is a great option for breakfast. High in anti-inflammatory omega-3, this sweet pudding is a make-ahead recipe that'll save you time during the morning rush. Simply mix together the ingredients the night before, pop it in the refrigerator and look forward to a special treat the next day—it's that simple. I have made this pudding many times over and never tire of it. You can change the liquids you use to soak the chia and change the toppings according to what's in season. A mixture of regular whole milk and honey topped with banana and almonds is another great combo.

Ingredients

⅔ cup/3½ oz/100 g white chia seeds
2 cups/17 fl oz/500 ml soy milk
1 x 400 ml can coconut milk
2 tablespoons honey
1 teaspoon ground cinnamon

7 oz/200 g natural (plain) yogurt
9 oz/250 g fresh strawberries, sliced
2 teaspoons white sesame seeds, toasted

Method

Place the chia seeds in a large bowl along with the soy, coconut, honey and cinnamon. Stir well to combine.

Cover and place in the refrigerator to soak for 3–4 hours, or overnight.

Stir in the yogurt to loosen the mixture and divide between serving bowls. Top the pudding with the sliced strawberries and scatter over the sesame seeds.

Notes

Alternatively serve this pudding with a fruit salad of sliced papaya, banana and limes. Or try it with fresh figs and pistachio nuts.

Prep: 15 minutes (plus soaking time)

Smoked Salmon, Soft Eggs & Herb Pesto

Serves 2

I used to have a healthy cooking segment on television that followed and reported on all the latest celebrity diets. It was during this time that I first made this dish. It's quick, healthy and easy to make—who doesn't love that in the morning?

Ingredients

4 small free-range eggs
1 tablespoon olive oil
2 bunches asparagus, trimmed
2 teaspoons fresh ginger, sliced
1 long red chilli, sliced
1 small avocado, peeled, seeded and sliced
9 oz/250 g smoked salmon

For the Herb Pesto

¼ cup/1 oz/30 g almonds
1 tablespoon each: chives, parsley, basil
1 tablespoon olive oil
Sea salt flakes and pepper
2 teaspoons lemon juice

Method

Place the eggs in a small pot of boiling salted water. Cook for 5–6 minutes for soft centres. Remove the eggs from the heat and place in a bowl of cold water to stop them from cooking. Peel and set aside.

Meanwhile, heat the oil in a non-stick frying pan set over a medium heat. Add the asparagus, ginger and chilli and grill (broil) for 2–3 minutes, adding a dash of water to help steam. Remove from the pan, keep warm and set aside.

To make the pesto: roughly chop the almonds on a large chopping board. Add the herbs, oil and season with salt and pepper. Continue to chop until a rough pesto or paste has formed. Squeeze over the lemon juice and stir in.

To serve, place the asparagus, ginger and chilli on the base of a serving plate. Top with the sliced avocado and smoked salmon. Break over the soft eggs and top with a spoonful of herb pesto. Crack over some black pepper and serve with extra lemon wedges.

Spiced Roast Pumpkin with Ricotta & Maple Bacon

Serves 4

This recipe's a delicious treat. It's a good dish to make over the weekend when you've got time to enjoy cooking. It's a beautiful twist on the traditional cooked breakfast.

Ingredients

1¾ fl oz/50 ml olive oil

2¼ lb/1 kg jap (kent) pumpkin, sliced into wedges, skin on

2 teaspoons ground cumin

1 teaspoon cinnamon

½ bunch (about 4 stems) kale, washed, stalks removed

8 rashers (strips) middle bacon

2 tablespoons maple syrup

1 cup /8 fl oz/250 ml Romesco sauce (see page 24)

7 oz/200 g fresh ricotta, roughly crumbled

2 oz/60 g hazelnuts, toasted and roughly chopped

Sea salt flakes and pepper

Method

Preheat the oven to 180°C/350°F/Gas mark 4. Drizzle 1 fl oz/30 ml of olive oil over the pumpkin and coat with the cumin, cinnamon and season with salt and pepper. Arrange the pumpkin on a lined baking tray and roast in the oven for 35–40 minutes, or until tender. Remove the pumpkin from the oven and allow to rest in a warm area.

Turn the oven up to 200°C/400°F/Gas mark 6. Place the bacon onto a lined oven tray and brush with the maple syrup. Bake the bacon for 10–12 minutes, or until golden and crisp, turning and brushing with more maple syrup as it cooks.

Meanwhile, heat the remaining oil in a non-stick frying pan and cook the kale with a pinch of sea salt for 2 minutes, or until wilted.

To serve, arrange the roast pumpkin on plates. Scatter over the kale and romesco sauce. Break over the maple bacon, ricotta and hazelnuts.

Rocket, Prosciutto & Parmesan Breakfast Salad

Serves 2

This dish offers a fabulous light and tasty start to the day. If you're not keen on heavy carbs first thing, give this one a whirl. Add some fresh, sliced pear if you like. You could even eat it for lunch.

Ingredients

4 free-range eggs

6 slices prosciutto

2 cups/10 oz/280 g baby rocket (arugula), washed

1 cup/1 ¼ oz/40 g radicchio leaves, washed

1¾ fl oz/50 g Parmesan, shaved

½ avocado, diced

1 teaspoon cracked black pepper

1 tablespoon extra virgin olive oil

1 tablespoon aged balsamic vinegar

2 teaspoons maple syrup

Method

Cook the eggs in a pan of boiling salted water for 6–8 minutes. Remove the eggs from the heat and place into a bowl of cold water. Once cool enough to handle, peel and set aside.

Heat a non-stick pan over a medium heat. Cook the prosciutto for 1–2 minutes each side, or until crispy. There should be enough fat on the prosciutto to cook, but add a little oil to your pan, if desired. Once the prosciutto is cool, break up into rough pieces.

Mix together the balsamic and maple syrup until combined.

To serve, arrange the rocket leaves, radicchio, Parmesan, avocado and prosciutto in serving bowls. Top with the cooked eggs, black pepper and drizzle over the balsamic dressing. Serve warm.

Chickpea Breaky Salad with Harissa & Feta Avocado

Serves 4

If you're after something a little bit different for breakfast or brunch, this dish will fit the bill. It's a great combination of creamy avocado, spicy harrissa, fresh mint and soft eggs rolled in crunchy dukkah. Smashing.

Ingredients

7 oz/200 g marinated Persian feta, drained and 1½ fl oz/ 40 ml of the oil reserved

1 large ripe avocado, peeled and roughly chopped

2 teaspoons harissa paste

1 tablespoon lemon juice, plus extra to serve

1 teaspoon brown sugar

¼ cup/2 tablespoons mint leaves, finely chopped, plus extra to serve

3 green zucchini (courgettes), sliced thinly lengthways

4 small free-range eggs

1 x 14 oz/400 g can chickpeas, drained and rinsed

¼ cup dukkah (see page 30)

Sea salt flakes and pepper

Method

Place the feta in a large bowl along with the avocado, harissa paste, lemon juice, brown sugar, mint and a good pinch of sea salt and pepper. Using the back of a fork, smash the ingredients together until just combined, but so there's still a few chunks of avocado. Be careful not to blend too much as you will end up with a puree. Set aside.

Heat a non-stick frying pan over a medium heat. Add ¾ fl oz/20 ml of the reserved oil and cook the zucchini, in batches for 1–2 minutes each side, or until just wilted. Remove the zucchini from the heat and set aside.

Bring a pan of salted water to the boil, add the eggs and simmer for 6–8 minutes. Drain the eggs from the water and place in a bowl of chilled water to cool. Once the eggs are cool enough to handle, peel and set aside.

Place the chickpeas, zucchini, remaining oil and a pinch of sea salt into a large bowl. Toss together and divide among serving plates. Place a large dollop of the smashed avocado on top of the chickpea salad and then break over the eggs. Sprinkle with dukkah, mint leaves and serve with extra lemon wedges.

Crisp Iceberg Salad with Green Goddess Dressing

Serves 4

Think of this as a quirky version of the traditional Caesar salad. The creamy, herby dressing I've used is also a great match for the crispy Iceberg lettuce, smoky pancetta and gooey eggs.

Ingredients

12 slices mild pancetta

4 free-range eggs

2 baby Iceberg or Cos lettuce, cut into thick wedges

1 medium red radicchio, washed and leaves torn

For the Green Goddess Dressing

1 anchovy fillet, drained

⅓ cup/5 oz/150 g quality garlic aioli

2 tablespoons thick Greek (strained plain) yogurt

½ small avocado

1 tablespoon chives, chopped, plus extra to serve

1 tablespoon parsley, chopped

10 basil leaves, picked

1 tablespoon lemon juice

Sea salt flakes

2 teaspoons honey

Method

Cook the pancetta in a non-stick frying pan set over a medium/high heat for 1–2 minutes each side, or until crisp and golden. Remove from the heat and drain on kitchen towel.

Cook the eggs in a pan of boiling salted water for 6–7 minutes, then refresh under cold water to cool. Peel the shell from the eggs, roughly chop and set aside.

Place the green goddess dressing ingredients into a food processor and blend until smooth.

To serve, place the iceberg wedges onto serving plates. Scatter over the radicchio, chopped eggs and break over the crisp bacon or pancetta. Drizzle over the dressing and garnish with chopped chives.

Asian Omelette with Cashew & Bean Sprout Salad

Serves 2

I love to add an Asian twist to my dishes even at breakfast time. If you find omelettes a bit heavy, try adding fresh herbs, spicy chilli and crispy beansprouts to lighten things up.

Ingredients

4 free-range eggs
2 teaspoons olive oil
White pepper
1 teaspoon fish sauce
1 teaspoon caster (superfine) sugar
¼ cup/2 fl oz/60 ml light (skimmed) milk
2 teaspoons sesame oil
½ bunch English spinach, washed and trimmed
2 cups/8 oz/200 g bean sprouts, washed
1¾ oz/50 g unsalted cashews
1 long red chilli, sliced
1 tablespoon oyster sauce
½ cup/4 tablespoons coriander (cilantro) leaves

Method

Lightly whisk 2 eggs in a bowl, add a pinch of pepper and half of the fish sauce, sugar and milk (reserving the other half for the second omelette).

Heat 1 teaspoon of the oil in a small non-stick frying pan over medium heat. Pour in the egg mixture and gently push the outer edges of the omelette into the centre for 1 minute. Once the egg is nearly set, remove it from the heat and fold one side of the omelette over. Remove from the pan. Set aside and keep warm while you repeat with the second omelette.

Meanwhile, heat the sesame oil in a small non-stick frying pan over medium heat. Cook the spinach for 2 minutes then stir in the beanshoots. Remove from the heat so they still retain some crunch.

To serve, place the omelettes onto a serving dish and top with the spinach, beanshoots, chilli, cashews, oyster sauce and coriander.

Charred Corn with Kale, Fried Egg & Jalapeno Salsa

Serves 2

The jalapeno salsa in this dish will add zing to your morning. Made fresh, it has a strong kick but will become milder over time, if made in advance. The combination of charred corn, creamy black beans, chewy kale and spicy salsa is divine.

Ingredients

For the Jalapeno Salsa:

1 tablespoon olive oil

5 jalapenos, sliced

½ small white onion

1 garlic clove

½ teaspoon sea salt

¼ cup/2 fl oz/60 ml white vinegar

1 tablespoon caster (superfine) sugar

1½ fl oz/40 ml olive oil

2 small corn cobs, kernels sliced off

4 stems curly kale, stalks removed, chopped

½ cup/4½ oz/125 g canned black beans (turtle beans) drained

2 large free-range eggs

½ teaspoon paprika

2 tablespoons crème fraiche

2 wholemeal (whole wheat) tortillas, warmed, to serve

Method

For the salsa, heat the oil in a small pan set over a medium heat. Add the jalapenos and cook for 3–4 minutes, then add the onion, garlic and salt and continue to cook for another 3–4 minutes. Add ⅓ cup/2 ¾ fl oz/80 ml of water, the vinegar and sugar and leave on a gentle simmer for 8–10 minutes, or until the liquid has reduced by half. Blend the salsa in a small food processor. Set aside.

Meanwhile, heat ¾ fl oz/20 ml of the olive oil in a non-stick pan set over a medium/high heat. Add in the corn kernels and a small pinch of sea salt. Cook the corn, stirring for 5 minutes, or until golden and cooked. Remove from the heat and keep warm. Place the same pan back onto the heat along with 2 teaspoons of the olive oil. Cook the kale along with a small pinch of sea salt for 2–3 minutes, or until wilted. Add the black beans and cook for 1 minute to warm through. Remove from the heat and keep warm. Place the pan back onto the heat with the remaining oil.

Fry the eggs for 3–4 minutes, or until cooked to your liking.

To serve, place the kale and black beans onto warm serving plates and top with the fried egg. Scatter over the corn, crème fraiche, paprika and jalapeno salsa. Serve with warm tortilla.

Crab, Corn & Green Onion Omelette

Serves 2

Sweet crab meat is a great partner for eggs. If ever there's crab omelette on the menu somewhere, I'll be sure to order it. I've made this dish a few times and the method is definitely easier than it sounds. Don't just reserve it for fancy nights out, have a go at cooking it at home, you might just impress yourself!

Ingredients

1¾ fl oz/50 ml olive oil

2 cobs corn

4 large free-range eggs

1 tablespoon fish sauce (nam pla)

2 teaspoons sesame oil

2 teaspoons caster (superfine) sugar

7 oz/200 g picked blue swimmer crab meat

2 green shallots, finely sliced

1 long green chilli, finely sliced

2 tablespoons oyster sauce

Sea salt flakes and pepper

Method

Heat 2 teaspoons of the oil in a non-stick frying pan set over a medium/high heat. Add the corn cobs along with a pinch of sea salt. Cook the corn, turning occasionally for 8–10 minutes, or until cooked through and slightly charred. Remove the corn from the heat and once cool enough, slice the kernels from the cob and set aside.

Whisk together the eggs, fish sauce, sesame oil and sugar.

Heat 20 ml of the olive oil in a non-stick frying pan over a medium heat. Pour in half the egg mixture and once the outer part of the omelette starts to cook, gently pull it into the centre of the pan and allow the runny egg to run to the outer part of the pan. Once the omelette is nearly set, scatter over half the corn and half of the crab. Leave on the heat for 1 minute to warm through. Remove from the heat and garnish with half the shallots, chilli and oyster sauce. Repeat with the remaining ingredients for the second omelette.

Potato, Bacon & Egg Salad

Serves 4

This dish is a modern take on traditional potato salad. My version is more of a meal than a side dish. I've added fresh celery for extra crunch, left the potatoes chunkier (to avoid them being drowned in the dressing) and included some yummy gooey eggs, which are always a good idea!

Ingredients

2¼ lb/1 kg baby potatoes, washed and skin on
4 free-range eggs
4 rashers (strips) rindless bacon
½ cup/3 oz/85 g celery, finely diced, yellow top leaves reserved for garnish
¼ cup/2 tablespoons chives, finely chopped
¼ cup/2 tablespoons flat leaf parsley, chopped
½ ripe avocado, peeled and sliced
½ cup/4 oz/115 g Greek (strained plain) yogurt
⅓ cup/2½ oz/75 g quality mayonnaise
1 tablespoon seeded mustard
1 tablespoon maple syrup
Sea salt flakes and ground white pepper

Method

Put the potatoes into a large pan and cover with cold water. Add a generous pinch of sea salt, place onto a medium heat and bring to the boil. Reduce the heat to a simmer and cook the potatoes for 8–10 minutes, or until just cooked through. Remove from the heat, drain and set aside.

Meanwhile, put the eggs in a pan of salted water, bring to the boil, then reduce the heat and simmer for 6–8 minutes. Remove the eggs from the heat and place in a bowl of chilled water to arrest cooking. Once cool enough to handle, peel the eggs and set aside.

Fry the bacon over a medium heat in a non-stick frying pan for 2–3 minutes each side, or until golden and crisp. Remove from the pan and drain on kitchen towel.

In a bowl, whisk together the yogurt, mayonnaise, mustard, maple syrup and a pinch of sea salt and ground white pepper.

Once the potatoes have cooled a little, cut them into quarters and place into a large bowl along with the celery and pour over the dressing. Gently toss to coat and arrange on a serving plate. Roughly tear the bacon into pieces and scatter over the top of the potatoes. Break the eggs into rough halves and add to the salad. Scatter over the sliced avocado, chives, parsley and reserved celery tops. Serve warm.

Crispy Fried Eggs with Xo Chilli & Sweet Soy Dressing

Serves 4

Kylie Kwong is one of my food heroes and this is my version of her recipe of fried eggs with chilli and oyster sauce. I've made it into a complete meal rather than a side dish. Ribbons of raw vegetable and handfuls of fresh herbs complement the crispy, oily eggs perfectly.

Ingredients

1¾ fl oz/50 ml tamari soy sauce

1 tablespoon brown sugar

1 cup/17 fl oz/500 ml sunflower oil

8 free-range eggs

1 gem lettuce, washed and roughly torn

2 green zucchini (courgettes), sliced into thin julienne strips

1 large carrot, sliced into thin julienne strips

1 cup mint, leaves picked

1 cup coriander (cilantro), leaves picked

½ cup/4 fl oz/125 ml my Xo chilli sauce (see page 23)

1 long red chilli, seeded and sliced into thin julienne strips

Method

Place the tamari, brown sugar and 1 fl oz/30 ml water into a small saucepan and place onto a medium heat. Stir to dissolve the sugar and bring to a gentle simmer. Cook for 4–5 minutes, or until the sauce has reduced by half and is syrupy. Remove from the heat and set aside.

Meanwhile, heat the oil in a wok, or large fry pan over a medium high heat. Working in batches, break each egg into a small bowl and carefully slide into the hot oil. Using a slotted spoon to move the egg around, cook for 1 minute, or until the egg is crisp and golden. Remove from the oil and drain on kitchen towel. Repeat with the remaining eggs.

Place the lettuce on the base of serving plates or bowls. Scatter over the zucchini, carrot and half of the mint and coriander leaves. Divide the eggs onto the salads and drizzle over the sweet tamari and Xo chilli sauce. Garnish with the remaining mint, coriander and red chilli.

Shaved Brussels, Pancetta
& Poached Egg Salad

Serves 2

As a kid, I hated sprouts and I've only started eating them again thanks to my partner's small obsession with them! Brussels don't always have to be boiled and served with a roast. In this salad, they're finely shaved and served raw. Thumbs up to the sprout!

Ingredients

7 oz/200 g Brussels sprouts, trimmed
1 tablespoon olive oil
6 slices pancetta
1 garlic clove, sliced
4 large brown mushrooms, sliced
¾ oz/20 g butter
2 cups/2 oz/60 g Cavalo nero (Tuscan kale) washed and roughly chopped
4 free-range eggs
1 tablespoon white vinegar
¼ cup/1 oz/30 g toasted hazelnuts, chopped

For the Dressing:

1 fl oz/30 ml olive oil
1 tablespoon aged balsamic vinegar
2 teaspoons maple syrup

Method

Using a mandolin, or sharp knife, thinly shave the sprouts. Set aside in a bowl.

Heat the olive oil in a non-stick frying pan set over a medium heat and cook the pancetta for 1–2 minutes each side, or until golden and crisp. Remove and drain on kitchen towel.

Place the same pan back onto a medium heat, retaining any oil from the pancetta. Add the garlic, mushrooms, butter and a pinch of sea salt and pepper. Cook, stirring for 3–4 minutes then add the cavalo nero and continue to cook for another 2–3 minutes. Remove from the heat and set aside.

To poach the eggs, bring a pan of salted water to the boil, add in the white vinegar and turn down to a very gentle simmer. Crack each egg into a small bowl before carefully sliding it into the water. Poach the eggs for 3–4 minutes, for soft centres. Remove with a slotted spoon and drain the eggs on kitchen towel.

Mix together the dressing ingredients in a small bowl and season.

To serve, toss the shaved Brussels with the mushroom mixture and divide into serving bowls. Break over the crisp pancetta and place on the poached eggs. Scatter over the hazelnuts and drizzle with dressing. Serve warm.

Ham & Eggs with Sweet Pea Pesto

Serves 2

This delicious recipe is my hipster take on Christmas leftovers. It's great eaten ANY time of the year though.

Ingredients

2 free-range eggs

2 cups/4 oz/115 g baby spinach

7 oz/200 g sliced leg ham

1 small avocado, peeled and halved

¼ cup/2 tablespoons chives, finely sliced

lemon wedges to serve

For the Pea Pesto:

1 cup/4 oz/115 g frozen peas, thawed

½ cup/2½ oz/75 g rocket (arugula) leaves, washed

¾ oz/20 g pine nuts

½ cup/4 tablespoons mint leaves

½ cup/4 tablespoons basil leaves

¾ oz/20 g Parmesan, fresh grated

2 tablespoon olive oil

Method

Place all the pesto ingredients into the bowl of a small food processor and blend until a smooth paste. Add a dash of warm water if the mixture is a little too dry. Set aside.

Put the eggs in a pan of salted water, bring to the boil and simmer for 6–8 minutes. Drain, then put the eggs in a bowl of cold water and once cool enough to handle, peel the eggs and set aside.

Cook the spinach in a small non-stick pan set over medium heat along with 1 tablespoon of water for 1–2 minutes, or until wilted.

Place the pea pesto onto the base of serving bowls. Top with the spinach, sliced ham, eggs, avocado, chives and lemon wedges.

Salmon and Quinoa Breakfast Bowl with Dukkah Eggs

Serves 2

Healthy ingredients are combined here for a spectacular superfood breakfast, brunch or lunch dish.

Ingredients

2 large free-range eggs

2 x 4½ oz/125 g salmon fillets, pin boned

1 fl oz/30 ml olive oil

2¾ oz/80 g Halloumi cheese, sliced in half

3 cups/3 oz/85 g curly kale, trimmed and sliced

⅔ cup/3½ oz/100 g white quinoa seeds

½ large avocado, peeled and quartered

2 tablespoons Dukkah (see page 30)

Lemon wedges, to serve

Sea salt flakes and pepper

Method

Place the quinoa into a pan and cover with 12 fl oz/350 ml cold water. Place over a medium-high heat and bring to a boil. Turn down the heat to a gentle simmer and cook, covered for 12–14 minutes, or until the liquid has been absorbed and the quinoa is light and fluffy. Remove from the heat, cover the quinoa to keep warm and set aside.

Put the eggs in a small pan, fill with water and a pinch of salt and bring to the boil. Reduce the heat to a simmer and continue to cook for 6–8 minutes. Plunge the eggs into a bowl of cold water to arrest cooking. Once cool enough to handle, peel off the shells and set aside.

Set a non-stick frying pan over a medium heat. Season the salmon with sea salt and pepper, and coat with half the oil. Cook the salmon skin side down for 3–4 minutes, or until crispy. Turn the salmon over and cook for another 2 minutes, or until the salmon is just cooked through. Remove the salmon from the heat, set aside and keep warm. The salmon will continue to cook while it is resting. Place the same pan back onto the heat and wipe out with a kitchen towel. Heat the remaining olive oil and fry the halloumi for 2 minutes on each side, or until golden. Remove from the pan and set aside. Return the pan to the heat and add the kale and a pinch of sea salt. Cook the kale, stirring for 2–3 minutes, or until just wilted.

To serve, place the cooked quinoa into the base of the serving bowls. Arrange the cooked salmon, kale, halloumi, avocado and lemon wedges on top. Add the eggs and sprinkle with the dukkah. Serve warm.

Green Bean Slaw with Eggs, Olive & Anchovies

Serves 4

I really like this recipe... Actually, I LOVE it! It's a fabulous combination of Mediterranean flavours and a quirky twist on traditional slaw.

Ingredients

1 lb 2 oz/500 g green beans, trimmed
4 small free-range eggs
1 small red onion, finely sliced
4 radishes, finely sliced into matchsticks
½ cup/3 oz/85 g small black olives, pitted and squashed
½ cup/4 tablespoons flat leaf parsley, chopped
1 can anchovies, drained

For the Dressing

¼ cup/2 oz/60 g Greek (strained plain) yogurt
¼ cup/2 oz/60 g quality mayonnaise
2 teaspoons Dijon mustard
2 teaspoons lemon zest
¾ fl oz/20 ml lemon juice
2 teaspoons honey

Method

Bring a large pan of salted boiling water to the boil. Cook the beans for 2 minutes then remove from the pan and plunge into a bowl of iced water to stop them cooking further. Slice the cold beans lengthways with a vegetable peeler or large knife into thin strips.

Bring another pan of salted water to the boil. Cook the eggs for 7 minutes, then remove them from the pan and place in a bowl of cold water. Peel off the shells when cool enough to handle, slice and set aside.

Place the beans, onion, radish, olives and parsley into a large bowl. Combine all the dressing ingredients, then pour over the beans and toss to mix thoroughly.

Place the bean salad onto serving plates and top with the eggs and anchovy fillets. Drizzle with a little extra olive oil and a crack of black pepper.

Dill Fritatta with Hot Smoked Salmon & Crème Fraîche

Serves 2

Fritattas are great for using up ingredients. I make this recipe on the fly. Sometimes a spontaneous fridge raid works wonders!

Ingredients

4 cups/8 oz/250 g baby spinach leaves

1 fl oz/30 ml olive oil

5 free-range eggs, lightly beaten

¼ cup/2 fl oz/60 ml milk

¼ cup/2 tablespoons dill, finely chopped

7 oz/200 g hot smoked salmon fillet

3½ oz/100 g crème fraiche

¼ cup/2 tablespoons chives, chopped

Lemon wedges, to serve

Sea salt flakes and ground black pepper

Method

Set a medium non-stick pan over a medium heat. Add the baby spinach along with 1 tablespoon of water and a pinch of sea salt. Cook for 1–2 minutes, or until wilted. Remove the spinach from the pan and set aside. Return the pan to the heat, wipe out with paper towel and add the olive oil. Mix together the eggs and milk and season with sea salt and pepper. Pour the eggs into the pan and gently cook for 3–4 minutes. Remove the skin from the hot smoked salmon fillet and roughly break up into flakes. Place the salmon and cooked spinach on top of the eggs. Cover the pan and continue to cook for 2–3 minutes, or until the eggs have set. Add a dollop of crème fraiche, the chives and a crack of black pepper. Serve warm with lemon wedges.

Freekeh and Shaved Brussels Salad with Herbed Eggs

Serves 4

Freekeh is green wheat that has been roasted during production. It cooks similar to brown rice, but is much higher in fibre and is packed with protein, making it a great ingredient for vegetarians. Whole freekeh cooks in around 40 minutes, while the cracked grain cooks in around 20 minutes. This grain absorbs other flavours, holds its shape very well and has a delicious nutty character.

Ingredients

5 oz/150 g cracked freekeh
4 free-range eggs
2¾ fl oz/80 ml extra virgin olive oil, plus extra for drizzling
½ bunch/2 stems kale, sliced
½ cup/2 oz/60 g roast almonds, chopped
10½ oz/300 g Brussels sprouts, very finely shaved
¼ cup/2 tablespoons parsley, finely chopped
¼ cup/2 tablespoons chives, finely sliced
1 ¼ fl oz/40 ml sherry vinegar
1 tablespoon honey
Sea salt flakes and pepper

Method

Cook the freekeh in a pan of boiling salted water for 20–25 minutes. Drain well and spread out on a flat tray to cool.

Cook the eggs in a pan of boiling salted water for 6–8 minutes, then drain and put the eggs into a bowl of chilled water. Once cool enough to handle, peel and set aside.

Heat ¾ fl oz/20 ml of the oil in a non-stick frying pan over medium heat. Add the kale and a pinch of sea salt and cook for 2–3 minutes until wilted. Remove from the heat and place into a large bowl with the freekeh, almonds and shaved Brussels srpouts.

For the dressing, whisk together the remaining oil with the sherry vinegar, honey and a pinch of sea salt until well combined, then pour over the freekeh salad. Toss well, then divide between serving bowls. Place the parsley and chives into a bowl and roll each egg in the herbs to coat before placing them on top of the salad. Drizzle with a little extra olive oil and serve.

Notes
Freekeh is available from larger supermarkets, health food stores or specialty food stores.
Substitute freekeh for brown rice, lentils or quinoa for a gluten-free option.

Seafood

Tuna Tataki Salad with Pickled Ginger & Fried Shallots

Serves 4 as part of a banquet

I first made this dish as a canapé. Since then I've converted it into my favourite salad. One small mouthful as a canapé just wasn't enough!!

Ingredients

10½ oz/300 g sashimi grade tuna fillet, left whole

2 teaspoons sesame oil

½ teaspoon sea salt

⅓ cup good quality pickled ginger

1 tablespoon tamari soy, plus extra to serve

2 teaspoons olive oil

1 tablespoon Japanese Kewpie mayonnaise

2 tablespoons Asian fried shallots

1 teaspoon black sesame seeds, toasted

1 teaspoon white sesame seeds, toasted

Baby micro herbs, or chives, to garnish

Method

Make sure the piece of tuna is an even size. If need be, slice the tuna in half to yield two even lengths.

Set a non-stick frying pan over high heat. Coat the tuna with the sesame oil and season with sea salt. Sear the tuna in the pan for 10 seconds on each side. Immediately transfer the tuna to a plate and freeze for 10 minutes. This will ensure the tuna does not continue to cook and will make it firm, making it easier to slice.

Remove from the freezer and slice the tuna into generous ⅛ in/½ cm pieces. Arrange the tuna onto a serving platter and top with the pickled ginger, tamari, olive oil, mayonnaise, fried shallots and sesame seeds and garnish with micro herbs.

Sashimi Salmon Salad with Yuzu & Ginger Dressing

Serves 2 as a light meal

I love the 'clean' flavours and simplicity of Japanese food. This recipe is great served with a green salad and takes mere minutes to whip up. All that's required is a trip to your local fish market to pick up the freshest salmon.

Ingredients

10½ oz/300 g Sashimi grade salmon, thinly sliced

1 tablespoon fresh ginger, peeled and sliced into fine julienne

2 teaspoons yuzu juice

1 teaspoon caster (superfine) sugar

1 tablespoon sesame oil

2 teaspoons tamari soy sauce

2 teaspoons olive oil

1 tablespoon chives, finely sliced

Method

Arrange the salmon in a single layer onto a serving plate and scatter over the ginger.

In a small bowl, dissolve the sugar in the yuzu juice, then mix in the tamari sauce. Set aside.

Place the sesame oil into a small saucepan over a high heat and bring to smoking point. Very carefully pour the hot sesame oil over the salmon to scald some of the flesh and the ginger.

Drizzle over the yuzu dressing, olive oil and top with the fresh chives. Serve immediately.

Notes

Yuzu juice is from the yuzu citrus plant, which originated in east Asia. The fresh fruit is difficult to source, but the bottled juice can be found in most Asian supermarkets.

BBQ Seafood & Watermelon Salad

Serves 6–8

I cooked this salad at one of my many cooking demonstrations. It was December, so the theme called for some easy Xmas inspired recipes. This dish is cooked in less than 30 minutes, and is both light and refreshing, leaving you with plenty of room for pudding!

Ingredients

½ cup/4 tablespoons fresh coriander (cilantro) leaves
2 teaspoons finely grated lemon zest
2 tablespoons lemon juice
2 tablespoons olive oil
1 long fresh red chilli, finely chopped
1 garlic clove, crushed
¾ cup/6 tablespoons fresh mint leaves
1 lb 2 oz/500 g large green shrimp, peeled and deveined
2 (about 14 oz/400 g) squid tubes, scored and cut into 2¾ in/6 cm pieces
2¼ lb/1 kg watermelon, rind removed, sliced into chunks
1 large avocado, sliced
1 Lebanese cucumber, peeled into ribbons
½ small red onion, thinly sliced

For the Dressing:

1 tablespoon extra virgin olive oil
2 tablespoons lemon juice
1 tablespoon honey
Sea salt flakes and pepper

Method

To the bowl of a food processor add ¼ cup/2 tablespoons of coriander, the lemon zest and juice, olive oil, chilli, garlic and ¼ cup/2 tablespoons of the mint and process until combined. Season with salt and pepper.

Combine the shrimp, squid and herb mixture in a glass bowl. Cover and place in the refrigerator for 10 minutes to marinate.

Meanwhile, to make the dressing whisk the oil, lemon juice and honey in a small bowl. Season and set aside.

Preheat a barbecue or chargrill on medium-high. Cook the shrimp and squid, in three batches, for 2–3 minutes, or until just cooked. Transfer to a plate. Cover with foil to keep warm.

Arrange the watermelon, avocado, cucumber, onion, prawns, squid, coriander and remaining mint on large platter. Drizzle over the dressing. Serve immediately.

Tuna, Edamame, Herb & Persian Feta Salad

SERVES 4

Sometimes the best meals are the simplest and this recipe is just that. It's the perfect dish for an entrée, although it'd also be great for a light weekend lunch dish. Add in a crisp glass of white... Hello weekend!

Ingredients

9 oz/250 g shelled edamame soybeans (frozen is fine)

9 oz/250 g frozen green peas

¼ cup/2 tablespoons chives, finely sliced, plus extra to garnish

¼ cup/2 tablespoons dill leaves, picked and chopped

¼ cup/2 tablespoons mint leaves, picked and chopped

1¾ fl oz/40 ml extra virgin olive oil

¾ fl oz/20ml lemon juice

1 teaspoon lemon zest

1 teaspoon honey

3½ oz/100 g marinated Persian feta, drained and crumbled

9 oz/250 g Sashimi grade tuna, sliced

Sea salt flakes and ground black pepper

Method

Bring a pan of salted water to the boil and cook the soybeans for 3 minutes, add in the frozen peas and cook for another 3 minutes. Drain and refresh the beans under running cold water to cool.

Place the cooled beans into a bowl with the chives, dill, mint and a pinch of sea salt and cracked black pepper.

Whisk together half of the oil with the lemon juice, lemon zest and honey. Pour the dressing over the beans, toss to coat and divide the beans between the serving bowls, then crumble the Persian feta over the top of the beans.

Toss the tuna slices with the remaining olive oil and a pinch of sea salt to season and place on top of the beans. Garnish with extra chives.

Note: Frozen edamame soybeans are from Asian supermarkets, or you can substitute for broad (fava) beans.

Asian Salmon Tartare with Avocado Mousse

Serves 4 as a starter

If you're cooking to impress, this dish is the perfect choice. The avocado mousse has a great textural element, elevating the dish to a true party pleaser!

Freeze the salmon for 20 minutes to firm it up, which will make slicing it much easier!

Ingredients

11 oz/300 g sashimi grade salmon fillet
¼ cup pickled ginger, finely diced
½ garlic clove, grated
⅓ cup/2 oz/60 g celery, finely diced, leaves reserved for garnish
1 small golden shallot, finely diced
1 long red chilli, seeds removed and finely diced
¼ cup/2 tablespoons coriander, finely chopped
1¾ fl oz/40 ml lime juice
1 teaspoon caster (superfine) sugar
2 teaspoons fish sauce (nam pla)
¾ fl oz/20 ml olive oil
1 teaspoon sesame oil
1 teaspoon black sesame seeds
1 tablespoon Asian-fried shallots, to serve
Baby coriander (cilantro) leaves, to garnish

For the Avocado Mousse

1 ripe avocado, peel and seed removed
2 teaspoons lime juice
4 fl oz/130 ml cream
Sea salt

Method

For the avocado mousse, blend the avocado, lime juice and a pinch of sea salt in a food processor until smooth and reserve in a bowl. Whip the cream until soft peaks form and gently fold into the avocado. Set aside in the refrigerator.

Finely dice the salmon into generous ⅛ in/½ cm cubes and place into a large bowl along with the ginger, garlic, celery, shallot, chilli and coriander.

Combine the lime juice, sugar, fish sauce, olive oil and sesame oil and stir until the sugar has dissolved. Pour over the salmon and toss well to coat.

To serve, place the salmon onto the base of the serving bowls. Spoon over the avocado mousse and scatter over the black sesame, fried shallots and baby herbs.

Note
Be careful not to dress the salmon too early with the dressing as the lime juice will start to cook the fish and it will change colour.

Tuna with Watermelon, Apple, Lime & Radish Vinaigrette

Serves 4

I love adding fruit to a salad to help freshen them up a little. With this dish, I've simply added apple and watermelon for texture and sweetness. These combine perfectly with salty olives and sour finger limes.

Ingredients

50 ml/1 ¾ fl oz rice vinegar
¾ oz/20 g caster (superfine) sugar
½ teaspoon sea salt flakes
1 teaspoon mirin
2 fl oz/60 ml olive oil
4 finger limes
½ cup watermelon, finely diced
¼ cup green apple, finely diced
2 red radish, finely diced
1 tablespoon chives, finely chopped
2¾ oz/80 g Kalamata olives, pitted and finely minced
9 oz/250 g sashimi-grade tuna, sliced
Micro cress, to garnish

Method

Whisk together the vinegar, sugar, salt, mirin and oil in a bowl.

Slice the finger limes in half lengthways, scoop out the pearls and add to the dressing along with the watermelon, apple, radish and chives.

Place the tuna onto a serving plate and spoon over the vinaigrette. Top with the black olives and garnish with micro cress.

Kingfish with Horseradish, Ginger & Spring Onions

Serves 2

More often than not sashimi is served with wasabi, In this dish I have replaced the wasabi with horseradish.

Ingredients

6 oz/180 g sashimi-grade kingfish, sliced

1 cup daikon radish, peeled and sliced into julienne strips

2 teaspoons fresh horseradish, finely grated

1 tablespoon light soy sauce

1 teaspoon sesame seeds, toasted

Ground white pepper

Baby coriander (cilantro), to garnish

For the Ginger and Spring Onion Dressing

1 ¾ oz/40 g fresh ginger, peeled and finely sliced

1 green spring onion (scallion), finely sliced

1 tablespoon coriander (cilantro) stems, washed and finely sliced

Sea salt flakes

1 teaspoon caster (superfine) sugar

1 ¾ fl oz/40 ml peanut oil

Method

For the dressing: pound the ginger, spring onion, coriander, pinch of salt and sugar into a paste in a mortar and pestle. Transfer to a heatproof bowl and mix well.

Heat the peanut oil in a small frying pan set over a medium/high heat. Carefully pour the hot oil over the paste, scalding the ingredients to release their fragrance, then mix well.

Arrange the daikon and kingfish on a serving plate. Spoon over the ginger dressing and pour over the soy sauce. Garnish with sesame seeds, white pepper and baby coriander.

Note

Fresh horseradish is not always available. Substitute for either horseradish in a jar or wasabi paste.

Thai BBQ Shrimp & Cashew Salad

Serves 4

This is food that is low on calories and high on freshness and flavour. Substitute the shrimp for any of your favourite BBQ meats, seafood or even tofu. This recipe offers a delicious combination of sweet shrimp, zesty dressing and creamy cashews.

Ingredients

20 large green king shrimp (jumbo prawns), peeled, de-veined, tail left on

1 tablespoon oil

2 garlic cloves, crushed

1 teaspoon ground black pepper

1 cup/4 oz/115 g unsalted roasted cashews, roughly chopped

1 Lebanese cucumber, seeded and thinly sliced

7 oz/200 g cherry tomatoes, sliced in half

3 spring onions (scallions), finely sliced

1 cup coriander (cilantro), chopped

1 cup Thai basil, leaves picked

2 cups/8 oz/250 g cellophane (glass) noodles soaked in hot water and drained

For the Dressing

Juice of 2 limes

1 tablespoon fish sauce (nam pla)

2 tablespoons palm/brown sugar

1 long red chilli, finely sliced

2 teaspoons sesame oil

Method

Heat a BBQ plate over a medium heat.

Combine the shrimp, oil, garlic and pepper in a bowl and toss to evenly coat.

Cook the shrimp for 1–2 minutes on each side, or until just cooked. Remove the shrimp from the heat and set aside to rest.

Meanwhile, in a large bowl, combine the cashews, cucumber, tomatoes, onions, coriander, Thai basil and glass noodles.

Mix all the dressing ingredients together in a bowl. Pour over the salad. Add the cooked shrimp and toss to coat evenly. Garnish with extra herbs. Serve immediately.

Green Tea Noodle Salad with Salmon & Ponzu

Serves 4

A few of my favourite Japanese ingredients have been combined in this recipe to create a good, hearty noodle salad! Ponzu dressing is Japanese. It's a citrus and soy-based dressing, using yuzu citrus. If you can't find yuzu, substitute with fresh lemon or lime. It tastes heavenly on most salads. It is also a great accompaniment to a fresh sashimi platter.

Ingredients

7 oz/200 g green tea soba noodles

3½ oz/100 g frozen podded edamame beans (soybeans)

1 tablespoon olive oil

5 oz/150 g baby spinach leaves

9 oz/250 g sashimi-grade salmon, sliced

1 ripe avocado, peeled and sliced

½ cup pickled ginger

1 tablespoon mixed black and white sesame seeds

¼ cup/2 tablespoons chives, finely sliced

For the Ponzu Dressing:

1 tablespoon yuzu

2 tablespoosn tamari soy sauce

1 tablespoon mirin

1 tablespoon rice wine vinegar

1 tablespoon brown sugar

1 teaspoon sesame oil

Ground white pepper

Method

Cook the green tea noodles in a pan of salted boiling water for 2–3 minutes. Drain and refresh under running cold water, then set aside.

Cook the edamame beans in a pan of salted boiling water for 3–4 minutes. Drain and refresh under running cold water, then set aside.

Heat the olive oil in a non-stick frying pan set over a medium heat. Add the spinach and a pinch of sea salt flakes and cook for 1–2 minutes, or until just wilted. Remove from the heat and set aside to cool.

Place the salmon onto a metal tray and using a kitchen blow torch, flame the salmon briefly until a few caramelised marks are visible, but the salmon has not cooked through.

In a bowl, whisk together all the ponzu dressing ingredients until the sugar has dissolved.

To serve, divide the noodles between the serving bowls and scatter over the edamame beans, spinach, avocado and pickled ginger. Add the salmon and spoon over the dressing. Garnish with the black and white sesame seeds and chives.

Notes

If you do not have a kitchen blow torch, just quickly sear the outside of the salmon in a hot pan for 5 seconds each side.

Green tea soba noodles, edamame beans and yuzu are from Asian supermarkets.

Steamed Shrimp Salad with Fragrant Oil Dressing

Serves 4 as a starter

Steaming prawns in their shell is a delicate way of cooking them and gives the flesh a melt-in-the-mouth texture.

Ingredients

20 large green (raw) king shrimp, shell on
½ cup/4 fl oz/125ml olive oil
2 garlic cloves, finely grated
1 tablespoon fresh ginger, finely grated
2 green spring onions (scallions) white part only, finely diced, green top reserved
1 tablespoon coriander (cilantro) stems, finely sliced, leaves reserved for garnish
1 tablespoon light soy sauce
1 tablespoon red wine vinegar
1 teaspoon caster (superfine) sugar
½ cup/3 oz/85 g celery heart, finely sliced
¼ cup/2 tablespoons Asian fried shallots
White pepper

Method

Remove the heads from the shrimp, but leave the shell on the body. Using a large sharp knife slice the shrimp in half lengthways and remove the intestine track.

To make the dressing, place the oil into a small heavy pan set over very low heat. Add the garlic, ginger, white parts of the onion, coriander stems and a small pinch of ground white pepper. Set aside for 15 minutes for the aromatics to infuse the oil. Ensure the oil does not get too hot as you are not cooking the aromatics, just supplying enough heat to release their fragrance. Remove the oil from the heat and stir in the soy, vinegar and sugar. Set aside.

Meanwhile, bring a large pan or wok of salted water to a gentle boil. Working in batches, place the shrimp in a single layer in a steamer basket and place over the boiling water and cook for 4–6 minutes, or until the shrimp are just cooked through.

Remove the shrimp from the steamer and arrange on a serving platter. Spoon over the fragrant oil and scatter with diced celery, sliced green spring onion tops, coriander leaves and fried Asian shallots. Serve warm.

Shrimp Cocktail with Spicy Marie Rose & Puffed Wild Rice

Serves 4

Different from the classic version, but I promise this is just as tasty! The rice in this dish adds a textural element and the sauce is Asian inspired. The crispy prawn crackers and sriracha chilli sauce also make all the difference to my classic twist!

Ingredients

1 cup/8 fl oz/250 ml sunflower oil

2 tablespoons black wild rice

8 dried prawn crackers*, optional

20 large green jumbo shrimp (king prawns), peeled and } de-veined

1 tablespoon olive oil, plus extra for drizzling

4 cups/4 oz/115 g gem lettuce, washed and chopped

1 ripe avocado, peeled and sliced

½ cup/4 oz/115 g quality mayonnaise

1 tablespoon tomato ketchup

2 teaspoons sriracha chilli sauce

2 tablespoon chives, finely sliced

20 small wooden skewers (for serving)

Method

Heat the sunflower oil to 160°C/325°F in a small pan. Tip the wild rice into the oil and fry for 2–3 minutes, or until puffed and crispy. Remove with a slotted spoon and drain on kitchen towel. In the same oil fry the dried prawn crackers until puffed and crispy. Drain on kitchen towel and set aside.

Place a small wooden skewer through the centre of each shrimp from the head to tail. This will stop the meat from curling when cooking.

Heat the olive oil to a medium heat in a non-stick frying pan. Season the shrimp with sea salt and pepper and cook for 2 minutes on each side, or until just cooked through. Remove the shrimp from the pan and allow to cool slightly before removing the wooden skewers.

Mix together the mayonnaise, tomato ketchup and sriracha chilli sauce.

To serve, place half the sauce onto serving plates. Top with lettuce, avocado and cooked shrimp. Drizzle with the remaining sauce and a little extra olive oil. Garnish with the puffed rice, chives and prawn crackers.

Note *Prawn crackers are available from Asian supermarkets. You can replace the crackers with Asian fried shallots.

Poached Chicken, Shrimp & Avocado Salad

Serves 4

Succulent poached chicken is paired with sweet shrimp and a tangy avocado dressing for my version of a very popular surf and turf dish!

Ingredients

2 x 6 oz/180 g skinless chicken breasts
1¾ pints/1 litre chicken stock
20 large cooked jumbo shrimp (king prawns), peeled, de-veined, tail left on
6 oz/180 g watercress, leaves picked
2 small baby Cos lettuce, inner leaves washed and torn
¼ cup/2 tablespoons chives, finely chopped

For the Avocado Yogurt:

1 ripe avocado
½ cup/4 oz/115 g plain Greek yogurt
¾ fl oz/20 ml lemon juice
2 teaspoons honey
Sea salt flakes

For the Dijon Dressing:

40 ml olive oil
1 teaspoon Dijon mustard
1 tablespoon lemon juice
2 teaspoons quality mayonnaise
1 teaspoon honey

Method

To poach the chicken, place the stock into a saucepan over a high heat. Bring the to the boil, then reduce the heat to a very gentle simmer. Place the chicken breast into the stock, cover and leave on a very low heat for 5 minutes. Turn the heat off and leave the chicken, covered, in the pan to poach for another 25 minutes. Remove chicken from the stock. Leave to cool then once cool enough to handle, slice into generous ⅛ in/½ cm strips.

Meanwhile, to make the avocado yogurt, place the avocado flesh, yogurt, lemon juice, honey and a pinch of sea salt in a small food processor. Blend until smooth and set aside.

To make the Dijon dressing, whisk all the ingredients together in a bowl with a pinch of sea salt and set aside.

To serve, divide the avocado yogurt between the serving plates and spread out using the back of a spoon. Arrange the watercress and lettuce on top. Scatter over the poached chicken and shrimp and drizzle with Dijon dressing and chopped chives

Baked Salmon & Zucchini Salad with Egg & Pickle Dressing

Serves 6

Think of this as a 'pimped-up' fish salad with tartar sauce! Substitute with portions of salmon if you can't find a whole side of salmon and swap the zucchini flowers with whatever vegetables are in season at the time. Grilled asparagus, ribbons of charred zucchini, or blanched broccolini work well.

Ingredients

3 lb 5 oz/1.5 kg whole skinless
   salmon side, pin-boned

1 tablespoon olive oil

18 whole zucchini (courgette)
   flowers

1 cup egg and pickle sauce
   (see page 17)

½ cup/4 tablespoons chives,
   with flowers if possible

18 garlic flowers (optional)

Sea salt and pepper

Method

Preheat the oven to 140°C/275°F/Gas mark 1.

Place the salmon on a lined oven tray, season with sea salt and bake for 25–30 minutes, or until just cooked through, but still tender in the centre. Remove the salmon from the oven and allow to rest for 5 minutes before transferring to a large, warmed serving platter.

Heat the oil in a large non-stick frying pan. Season the zucchini flowers with sea salt and grill (broil) for 2 minutes each side. Remove the zucchini flowers from the heat and arrange alongside the salmon. Finely chop the chives and scatter them over the salmon along with the garlic flowers, if using. Serve warm with the egg and pickle sauce on the side.

Honey Smoked Salmon, and Garlic, Chive & Mint Slaw

Serves 2

I made this recipe up on the spot one day while doing a cooking demonstration. I was given hot smoked salmon to cook and this was the result. What's more, the smoked salmon is store bought so it's easy and quick to make!

Ingredients

3 cups/9½ oz/ 270 g savoy cabbage, finely shaved

½ cup/4 ¾ oz/130 g zucchini (courgettes), sliced into julienne

½ cup/2½ oz/75 g carrot, sliced into julienne

¼ cup/2 tablespoons garlic chives, sliced

¼ cup/2 tablespoons fresh mint, chopped

7 oz/200 g hot honey smoked salmon, skin removed and flaked

For the Dressing:

1 tablespoon Kewpie mayonnaise

1 tablespoon lemon juice

1 teaspoon sesame oil

1 teaspoon fish sauce (nam pla)

1 teaspoon brown sugar

Pinch ground white pepper

Method

Mix all the dressing ingredients together in a large bowl. Add in the cabbage, zucchini, carrot, garlic chives, mint and salmon. Using clean hands toss the salad well to combine.

To serve place, divide the salad between the serving bowls.

Warm Salmon, Fennel & Orange Salad

Serves 4

The liquorice flavour of fresh fennel pairs well with any citrus. This is another super-healthy recipe and a great way to make an expensive ingredient like salmon go a long way.

Ingredients

2 oranges, segmented, with juice reserved

2 tablespoons lemon juice

2 tablespoons olive oil

1 tablespoon honey

2 baby fennel bulbs, shaved

14 oz (400 g) can chickpeas, drained

½ cup/4 tablespoons flat leaf parsley

½ cup/4 tablespoons dill

2 x 7 oz/200 g fresh Atlantic skinless salmon fillets, pin boned

2 cups/10 oz/280 g rocket (arugula) leaves

Salt and pepper

Method

Place the reserved orange juice in a bowl and mix together with the lemon juice, olive oil, honey and a pinch of salt and pepper. Add in the orange segments, shaved fennel, chickpeas, parsley and dill. Toss to coat with the dressing and set aside.

Heat a non-stick frying pan over medium heat. Season the salmon and fry for 2–3 minutes each side. Remove from the heat and allow to cool.

Place the rocket leaves on the base of a large serving platter. Top with the fennel salad mixture. Break over the cooled salmon and garnish with extra dill and lemon wedges.

Asian Pickled Cucumber, Calamari & Mushroom Salad

Serves 2

In this Asian-inspired salad, the crunchy pickled cucumbers work particularly well with the warm chewy calamari. Using a variety of mushrooms will give extra texture and make the taste more exotic.

Ingredients

2 Lebanese cucumbers, peeled

1 teaspoon sea salt flakes

1 teaspoon brown sugar

10½ oz/300 g fresh whole calamari

1¾ fl oz/40 ml extra virgin olive oil

1 garlic clove, finely sliced

5 oz/150 g mixed exotic mushrooms

2 long red chillies, seeds removed, and thinly sliced into julienne strips

1 green spring onion (scallion), thinly sliced into julienne strips

1 cup/8 tablespoons coriander (cilantro), leaves picked

1 tablespoon sesame seeds, toasted

For the Dressing:

1 tablespoon rice wine vinegar

1 tablespoon light soy sauce

1 tablespoon brown sugar

1 teaspoon sesame oil

½ teaspoon chilli oil

White pepper

Method

Cut the cucumbers in half lengthways and scoop out the seeds with a spoon. Place cut side down on a chopping board and slice on the diagonal into ½ in/1 cm slices. Place the cucumber slices in a bowl, sprinkle with sugar and salt and mix well. Cover and refrigerate for 30 minutes.

Meanwhile, to clean the calamari, gently pull the head and tentacles away from the body and discard the entrails. Remove the purple skin from the body, then trim the 'wings' from the body and set aside. Pull out the clear quill (backbone) from the body, then rinse the body, tentacles and wings and pat dry with kitchen towel. Cut the calamari into ½ in/1 cm strips.

Whisk together all the dressing ingredients in a large bowl.

Drain the cucumbers of any excess liquid and add them to the dressing along with the chillies and shallots and mix to coat. Set aside.

Heat ¾ fl oz/20 ml of the oil in a non-stick frying pan set over a medium heat. Add the mushrooms and stir-fry for 2 minutes. Add the garlic and a small pinch of sea salt and cook for another 1 minute. Remove the mushrooms from the pan and set aside.

Wipe out the frying pan with kitchen towel and place it over high heat. Add the remaining oil. Season the calamari with a pinch of sea salt and cook, stirring for 1–2 minutes, or until the calamari is just cooked, but still tender.

To serve, place half of the coriander leaves onto the base of a serving dish. Arrange the cooked mushrooms, cucumber mixture and calamari on top of the coriander. Garnish with the sesame seeds and remaining coriander leaves. Serve immediately.

Seared Tuna Nicoise with Pickled Onion & Pomme Frites

Serves 2

There are many versions of nicoise salad. This particular salad is a refined dish, made using fresh tuna steak, heirloom tomatoes, crisp radishes and golden French fries... C'est magnifique!

Ingredients

5 oz/150 g French (green) beans

2 free-range eggs

2 medium Sebago potatoes, cut into thin chips

400 ml/14 fl oz sunflower oil, for frying

2 x 5½ oz/160 g tuna steaks

1 tablespoon olive oil

5 oz/150 g heirloom cherry tomatoes, halved

2 red radish, finely sliced

8 black olives, pitted and crushed

10 basil leaves, picked

10 tarragon leaves, picked

For the Pickled Onion:

1 small red onion, finely sliced

½ teaspoon sea salt

2 teaspoons sugar

1 tablespoon sherry vinegar

For the Dressing:

1 anchovy

1 teaspoon baby capers

4 black olives

1 teaspoon seeded mustard

1 tablespoon sherry vinegar

2 teaspoons honey

1 fl oz/30 ml olive oil

Method

To pickle the onion, place all the ingredients into a bowl, stir to dissolve, cover and leave to pickle for 30 minutes.

Blanch the beans in a pot of salted boiling water for 2 minutes, remove from the water, refresh under cold running water and set aside. Place the same pot of water back onto the heat and bring to a boil. Cook the eggs for 6–8 minutes, drain and refresh under cold water. Peel and set aside.

Heat the sunflower oil to 160°C/325°F. Pat the chips dry with kitchen towel and fry for 5–6 minutes, or until golden and crisp, season, then drain on kitchen towel.

Meanwhile, coat the tuna in the olive oil and heat a non-stick frying pan over a high heat. Cook the tuna on one side only for 30–40 seconds. Remove from the heat and set aside.

For the dressing, place the anchovy, capers and olives on a board and chop into a rough paste. Mix together in a bowl with the mustard, vinegar, honey and olive oil.

To serve, place the tuna on the base of a serving plate. Scatter over the green beans, tomatoes, radishes, olives, basil leaves and tarragon. Break over the eggs, drizzle with the dressing and place on the pomme frites.

Octopus, Fennel & Lemon Salad

Serves 2

I love this dish! The Octopus takes a while to cook, but let me tell you, it's well worth the wait. The liquorice flavour of the fennel works really well with soft octopus and zingy lemon. For added enjoyment, add a cold glass of white wine and pretend you're soaking up the Mediterranean sun!

Ingredients

1 octopus, around 1 lb 6 oz/600 g

1 carrot, roughly chopped

½ brown onion, roughly chopped

2 bay leaves

1 garlic clove, skin on, lightly bruised

10 black peppercorns

¼ bunch/2 tablespoons parsley, chopped

1 medium sized fennel, shaved, green tops reserved

1 teaspoon lemon zest

1 tablespoon lemon juice

1 long red chilli, seeds removed, finely sliced

½ teaspoon sea salt flakes

½ teaspoon ground white pepper

1 tablespoon olive oil

Method

Remove the beak and eyes from the octopus. Wash under cold water and place it into a pan with the carrot, onion, bay leaves, garlic, pepper and parsley. Cover with cold water, season with a generous pinch of sea salt and place over a medium heat. Bring to a boil, then reduce the heat to a gentle simmer, cover and cook for 1½ hours, or until the octopus is tender. Remove the octopus from the stock and allow to cool slightly before placing onto a clean piece of muslin. Roll the octopus into a tight sausage and secure the ends with string. Roll in foil and refrigerate for 6 hours or overnight to set. Remove the octopus from the cloth and slice into thin rounds.

Arrange the shaved fennel onto the base of a serving platter. Place the sliced octopus on top of the fennel and scatter over the lemon zest, lemon juice, chilli, salt, pepper, olive oil and reserved green fennel tops.

Calamari Salad with Grilled Zucchini, Lemon & Fried Mint

Serves 4

Italian inspired, this dish is a little bit different. When buying calamari, make sure you get the freshest of fresh for best results.

Ingredients

⅔ cup/5½ fl oz/160 ml olive oil

½ cup/4 tablespoons mint leaves, picked

4 medium zucchini (courgettes), sliced thinly lengthways

1 lb 6 oz/600 g calamari, cleaned, cut into ¾ in/2 cm strips

2 garlic cloves, finely chopped

1 long red chilli, seeds removed, finely chopped

Zest of 1 lemon

1 lemon, sliced into quarters

4½ oz/120 g baby rocket (arugula) leaves

1 tablespoon sweet balsamic glaze

Sea salt flakes

Note
Sweet balsamic glaze is from selected supermarkets and specialty food stores.

Method

Pour the oil into a small pan or frying pan and set over medium heat. Once the oil is 160°C/325°F, carefully place the mint leaves into the oil and fry, in batches for 10–15 seconds, or until crisp. Be careful as the moisture in the leaves may make the oil spit. Remove with a slotted spoon and drain the leaves on kitchen towel and let the oil cool.

Heat a large non-stick frying pan and set it over a medium/high heat.

Place the zucchini into a large bowl and pour over 2 tablespoons of the oil used to cook the mint and a pinch of sea salt. Toss to coat then fry the zucchini in batches for 2 minutes on each side, or until cooked through. Place the zucchini onto a tray and set aside.

Wipe the large frying pan clean with kitchen towel and place over a high heat.

Put the calamari in a large bowl and season with a pinch of sea salt flakes and toss with the garlic, chilli and 1⅓ fl oz/40ml of the reserved oil used to cook the mint. Cook the calamari, in batches for 2–3 minutes, or until it is just cooked but still tender. Remove the calamari from the heat and sprinkle the lemon zest over the calamari while it is still hot.

To serve, place the rocket onto the base of a large serving platter. Scatter over the zucchini and top with the cooked calamari. Garnish with the fried mint leaves, balsamic glaze and lemon wedges. Serve immediately.

Scallop, Pickled Apple, Avocado & Speck Salad

Serves 4

The sweet and smoky combination of scallops and speck work well with fresh pickled apple. This is a great served as an entrée or impressive light lunch.

Ingredients

For the Avocado Puree:

1 ripe avocado, peeled and
   seed removed
1 tablespoon lemon juice
1 tablespoon quality
   mayonnaise
Sea salt flakes

For the Pickled Apple:

1 green apple, sliced into thin
   matchsticks
1 fl oz/30 ml white wine vinegar
1 tablespoon honey

7 oz/200 g piece speck, rind
   removed and cut into batons
24 scallops, cleaned
1¾ fl oz/40 ml olive oil
2 teaspoon seeded mustard
2 cups/4 oz/115 g watercress
   leaves, picked and washed

Method

To make the avocado puree, place the avocado, lemon juice, mayonnaise and a pinch of sea salt into the bowl of a small food processor and blend until it forms a smooth puree and set aside.

To lightly pickle the apple, whisk the vinegar, honey and a pinch of salt in a non-reactive bowl. Add the apple, gently toss and set aside for 10 minutes.

Meanwhile, heat a non-stick frying pan over a medium heat and cook the speck, stirring for 8–10 minutes, or until most of its fat has rendered and it is crisp and golden. Remove the speck and drain it on kitchen paper. Wipe the pan clean with kitchen paper and replace it over a medium-high heat. Add ¾ fl oz/20 ml of the olive oil. Season the sea scallops with salt and pepper and fry in the oil in batches for 30 seconds to 1 minute each side, or until they are golden on the outside but still translucent in the middle.

Drain the pickling liquid from the apple and place into a bowl. Whisk the seeded mustard and remaining olive oil to the pickle mixture for the dressing.

To serve, spoon the avocado puree onto serving plates and top with the scallops and speck. Scatter over the pickled apple and watercress leaves. Spoon over the mustard dressing and serve immediately.

Note
Scallops pair well with most cured meats. Try substituting Spanish chorizo, bacon, prosciutto or pancetta if you can't get speck.

BBQ Fish Salad with Fennel, Tomatoes & Olives

Serves 4

A light and low-carb meal, this is a delicious recipe for a weekend brunch or mid-week dinner. Flaky fish, fresh herbs, sweet tomatoes and crunchy fennel form a moreish combination!

Ingredients

2 tablespoons lemon juice, plus extra to serve

2 fl oz/60 ml extra virgin olive oil

1 teaspoon brown sugar

1 medium fennel bulb, trimmed and finely shaved and fronds reserved

14 oz/400 g white skinless fish fillets such as snapper, bream, barramundi

2 teaspoons finely grated lemon zest

¼ cup/2 tablespoons fresh marjoram, leaves picked and roughly chopped

4 ripe heirloom tomatoes, roughly chopped

½ cup/3 oz/85 g small mixed olives, pitted and crushed

¼ cup/2 tablespoons fresh basil leaves, finely sliced

Sea salt flakes and freshly cracked black pepper

Method

Place the lemon juice, ¾ fl oz/20 ml of olive oil, sugar and a pinch of sea salt flakes into a large non-reactive bowl. Add in the shaved fennel, toss to coat and set aside to lightly pickle for 20 minutes.

Meanwhile, heat a large non-stick frying pan over medium heat. Coat the fish in ¾ fl oz/20 ml of olive oil, half the marjoram leaves and lemon zest and season with cracked black pepper and sea salt. Cook the fish for 2–3 minutes on each side, or until cooked through. This will depend on the thickness of the fish fillets you are using. Remove the fish from the heat and set aside to rest and slightly cool.

Toss together the tomatoes, olives, basil leaves and season before placing onto serving plates or bowls. Drain any excess liquid from the fennel and place on top of the tomato mixture. Flake the fish into rough pieces and scatter over the top of the salads along with the remaining marjoram leaves, fennel fronds and drizzle with olive oil. Serve warm with extra lemon wedges.

Warm Crab Salad with Roast Tomato Thai Dressing

Serves 4

Although messy to eat, this dish is certainly worth the effort to make at home. Freshly cooked blue swimmer crab is known for its sweet flesh, which works really well with the aromatic, roast tomato dressing.

Ingredients

For the Roast Tomato Thai Dressing:

7 oz/200 g cherry tomatoes

1¾ fl oz/50 ml extra virgin olive oil

1 tablespoon ginger, peeled and chopped

2 long red chillies, seeds removed and roughly chopped

1 garlic clove, roughly chopped

1 tablespoon coriander (cilantro) stems, chopped

1 tablespoon brown sugar

1 tablespoon fish sauce (nam pla)

1½ fl oz/40 ml lime juice, plus extra to serve

4 medium fresh blue swimmer crabs

4 cups/8 oz/250 g iceberg lettuce, shaved

5 oz/150 g cherry tomatoes, halved

1 cup/8 tablespoons coriander (cilantro) leaves, picked

1 cup/8 tablespoons Thai basil leaves, picked

½ cup/4 tablespoons Vietnamese mint

¼ cup/2 tablespoons Asian fried shallots

Sea salt flakes

Method

Preheat the oven to 180°C/350°F/Gas mark 4. Place the tomatoes onto a lined oven tray, drizzle with the olive oil and season with a pinch of sea salt flakes. Roast uncovered for 20–25 minutes, or until caramelised.

Meanwhile, place the ginger, chillies, garlic, coriander and ½ teaspoon black pepper in a mortar and pestle and pound to form a paste. Add in the sugar, roasted tomatoes along with any juices, and gently bruise the tomatoes into the paste. Stir in the fish sauce and lime juice and taste to check the seasoning. Adjust if required and set aside.

Cook the crabs in a large pan of salted boiling water for 10–12 minutes. Drain the crabs and refresh under cold running water to cool them slightly. Clean the crabs by pulling off the back shell and removing the filters and wash away any impurities.

Cut the crabs into 4 even pieces and toss in a large bowl with the roast tomato dressing while the crabs are still warm.

To serve, place the iceberg lettuce onto serving plates and arrange the crab on top, along with any excess dressing. Scatter over the tomatoes, coriander, Thai basil, Vietnamese mint and fried shallots. Serve warm with extra lime wedges.

Tuna Salad with Crispy Potato, Poached Eggs & Basil Sauce

Serves 2

Similar to a nicoise salad but with a few tweaks! I've 'pimped-up' the poached eggs with a fragrant basil sauce, which acts as a healthy `sort-of` hollandaise!

Ingredients

7 oz/200 g kipfler potatoes

1 tablespoon white vinegar

2 free-range eggs

1 bunch/1 lb/450 g asparagus, trimmed

2 tablespoons olive oil

6 oz/180 g can yellow fin tuna in oil, drained

1 large heirloom tomato, sliced

8 black olives, pitted

1 tablespoon chives to serve

Sea salt flakes and ground black pepper

For the Basil Sauce:

1 cup/8 tablespoons basil leaves, picked

1 tablespoon dill, chopped

½ cup/4 oz/125 g plain Greek (strained plain) yogurt

1 tablespoon quality mayonnaise

1 tablespoon lemon juice

2 teaspoons honey

Method

For the basil sauce, place all the ingredients into a small food processor, season and blend until smooth. Set aside.

Place the potatoes into a pan, cover with cold water and add a pinch of sea salt. Put onto a medium heat and bring up to a simmer. Cook the potatoes for 6–8 minutes, or until just tender. Drain and refresh under chilled water to cool. Slice the potatoes in half lengthways and set aside.

For the eggs, place a pot of salted water over a medium heat and add in the vinegar. Bring up to a gentle simmer, before cracking each egg into a small bowl. Carefully slide both eggs into the water and leave to poach on a very gentle heat for 4–5 minutes. Remove the eggs from the pot with a slotted spoon and set aside.

Meanwhile, heat the olive oil over a medium heat in a non-stick frying pan and fry the potatoes for 2–3 minutes on each side, or until golden and crispy. Drain the potatoes on kitchen towel. Place the same pan back onto the heat, add the asparagus and a pinch of sea salt and fry for 2–3 minutes. Remove from the heat and set aside.

To serve, place the crispy potatoes onto the base of a serving plate. Arrange the asparagus, tuna, tomato and olives on top of the potatoes. Carefully top with the poached eggs, a large dollop of the basil sauce, chives and a pinch of ground black pepper. Serve warm.

Tomato Carpaccio with Ortiz Anchovy & Sourdough Crumbs

Serves 2

This dish relies on a handful of really good quality ingredients: sweet, ripe tomatoes, meaty anchovies and beautiful, crispy sourdough crumbs. These elements all make for a simple and flavourful lunch dish!

Ingredients

1 tablespoon olive oil
½ cup/1½ oz/45 g fresh sourdough crumbs
1 teaspoon fresh thyme leaves, picked
1 teaspoon lemon zest, finely grated
2 medium heirloom tomatoes, thinly sliced
6 ortiz canned anchovies, roughly broken with 1 tablespoon of oil reserved
6 fresh basil leaves, picked and finely sliced
Micro parsley, to garnish
Sea salt flakes and ground black pepper

Method

Heat the olive oil in a small pan set over medium heat and add the breadcrumbs, thyme and a small pinch of sea salt. Cook, stirring for 4–5 minutes, or until the crumbs are golden and crispy. Remove from the heat and mix through the lemon zest. Set aside.

Arrange the thinly sliced tomato on a large serving plate. Scatter over the anchovies, a small pinch of sea salt and a grind of black pepper. Drizzle over 1 tablespoon of reserved oil from the anchovies. Finish with the toasted crumbs, fresh basil and baby parsley.

Notes

Ortiz anchovies are fished from northern Spanish waters in spring. They are slowly cured in salt for 5 months before being hand filleted and packed into oil. These anchovies are traditionally and painstakingly prepared, hence the price tag (worth it though). Plump and intense in flavour, they are an exquisite delicacy and a perfect match for fragrant tomatoes.
Quality white anchovies are a good alternative if you cannot get Ortiz.

Tuna & Asparagus Salad with Brown Rice & Sumac Dressing

Serves 4

I've cooked this dish at several of my cooking demonstrations and it seems to tick all the boxes with the viewers. It's tasty, easy to make and healthy. Feel free to replace the brown rice with any of your favourite grains.

Ingredients

1 cup/7 oz/200 g brown rice

4 free-range eggs

2 bunches asparagus

2 x 7 oz/200 g tuna steaks

2¾ fl oz/80 ml extra virgin
   olive oil

1¾ fl oz/50 ml red wine vinegar

1 tablespoon ground sumac

1 tablespoon honey

2 green spring onions
   (scallions), finely sliced

1 cup/8 tablespoons flat leaf
   parsley, finely sliced

½ cup/3 oz/85 g green olives,
   pitted

⅓ cup/1½ oz/45 g pine nuts,
   toasted

Sea salt flakes

Method

Bring a large pan of water up to the boil, add in the brown rice and cook for 30 minutes, or until the grains are tender. Drain and keep warm.

Meanwhile, boil the eggs in salted water for 6–8 minutes. Remove from the boiling water and place in a bowl of cold water. Once cool to the touch, peel the eggs and set aside.

Blanch the asparagus in salted boiling water for 2 minutes. Remove from the heat and, once cool enough to touch, cut the asparagus in half lengthways.

Heat ¾ fl oz/20 ml of the oil in a non-stick frying pan set over a medium heat. Season the tuna with sea salt and black pepper. Cook for 1 minute each side then remove from the heat, set aside and keep warm.

Mix together the remaining oil, vinegar, sumac, honey and a generous pinch of sea salt. Pour half the dressing over the warm rice and stir in the spring onions and parsley. Place the rice onto the base of serving bowls. Slice the tuna into ½ in/1 cm slices and place on top of the rice along with the asparagus, green olives, remaining dressing and break over the eggs. Garnish with pine nuts and extra sumac. Serve warm.

Poultry

Quail, Smoked Eggplant, Quinoa & Harissa Yogurt Salad

Serves 4

This salad is perfect for serving for a special occasion. The spicy quail, smoky eggplant and creamy yogurt are a heavenly mix. Feel free to replace the quail with chicken or even lamb if you want something a bit more casual.

Ingredients

400 ml/14 fl oz chicken stock

3½ oz/100 g mixed quinoa seeds

2 medium eggplant (aubergine)

1 tablespoon ras el hanout*

6 quails, butterflied

1¾ fl oz/50 ml olive oil

1 red onion, finely sliced

½ cup/4 tablespoons mint leaves, torn

½ cup/4 tablespoons coriander (cilantro) leaves, torn

¼ cup/1½ oz/45 g pomegranate seeds

For the Harissa Yogurt:

1 cup/8 oz/250 g Greek (strained plain) yogurt

2 teaspoons harissa paste

1 tablespoon lemon juice

2 teaspoons brown sugar

*Ras el hanout is a spice mix from North Africa. You can find it in specialty food stores, spice shops and delicatessens.

Method

Place the quinoa and stock into a pan set over medium heat. Bring to the boil, cover and reduce the heat to a simmer. Cook the quinoa for 12-14 minutes, or until the water has been absorbed and the quinoa is light and fluffy. Stir with a fork to separate the quinoa before setting aside to cool. While the quinoa is cooking, put the whole eggplant onto the open flame of a gas cooktop and grill for 10 minutes, turning occasionally, burning the skin to get a good smoky flavour (see note). When the eggplant feels soft and starts to collapse, take off the heat and leave to cool. Scoop out and roughly chop the flesh. Set aside.

Combine the ras el hanout and 1 fl oz/30 ml olive oil in a bowl. Add the quail and toss to coat in the mixture. Set aside for 10 minutes to marinade. Heat remaining oil in a non-stick frypan over a medium heat and cook the onions with a pinch of sea salt for 6–8 minutes, or until onion is golden and almost crisp. Remove from the pan and set aside.

Preheat a non-stick frying pan over a medium/high heat. Cook the quail in batches for 2–3 minutes each side until browned and cooked through. Cover with foil and set aside to rest for 5 minutes. Combine all the yogurt ingredients together in a bowl. To serve, place the quinoa and smoked eggplant onto the base of the serving bowls. Dress with half of the harissa yogurt and top with quail, onions, mint, coriander, the remaining yogurt and the pomegranate seeds.

Note: Don't be afraid to try this technique. If you do not have a gas cooktop, char the eggplant under the grill in your oven. Set your grill to a high heat, grill the eggplant, turning occasionally for 10-12 minutes or until the skins have charred and the flesh is soft.

Asian Turkey Lettuce Cups

Serves 4–6 as a starter

I love putting food in lettuce cups, it's a great low-carb vessel to wrap your hands around and get stuck into! Turkey mince isn't always readily available but this dish will work just as well with chicken, pork or beef mince.

Ingredients

3½ oz/100 g vermicelli noodles

2 tablespoons vegetable oil

4 green spring onions (scallions), finely sliced

1 tablespoon ginger, grated

1 lb 2 oz/500 g turkey mince (or leftover roast turkey, shredded)

2 celery stalks, diced

¼ cup/2 fl oz/60 ml thick sweet soy sauce, (kecap manis), plus extra to serve

8 oz/225 g can water chestnuts, drained and chopped

1 medium carrot, peeled and grated

2 teaspoons sesame oil

8 lettuce leaves, (baby Cos or Iceberg), washed and trimmed

¼ cup/2 tablespoons coriander (cilantro) leaves

1 long red chilli, seeds removed and finely chopped

¼ cup/1 oz/30 g roasted crushed peanuts

Method

Soak the noodles in the boiling water for 5 minutes, or until soft, then drain. Cut into 2 in/5 cm lengths. Set aside.

Heat the oil in a frying pan set over high heat. Add the spring onions, ginger, celery and turkey mince and cook for 6–8 minutes, or until browned, breaking up any lumps with the back of a wooden spoon. Add in the sweet soy sauce, water chestnuts, carrot and sesame oil. Cook for another 3–4 minutes before stirring in the noodles to warm through.

Arrange the lettuce onto a large platter and spoon the mince mixture into lettuce cups and top with coriander, chopped chilli and nuts, then drizzle with a little extra sweet soy sauce.

Roast Market Vegetable Salad with Spiced Chicken

Serves 4

This dish is a great winter warmer and a good way to make vegetables the real hero of the dish.
I like to serve this on a big wooden board, plonked in the middle of the table.

Ingredients

1 bunch (about 4 medium) golden beetroot, washed, trimmed

1 lb/450 g pumpkin, cut into wedges

11 oz/300 g baby (Dutch) carrots, washed, trimmed

1 red onion, cut into wedges

2 cups/6 oz/175 g broccoli florets

4 large brown mushrooms, sliced

3½ fl oz/100 ml olive oil

1 lb 2 oz/500 g chicken breast, trimmed

2 teaspoons ground cumin

1 teaspoon ground cinnamon

1 cup/8 fl oz/250 ml tahini yogurt (see page 16)

1 small lemon, to serve

¼ cup/1 oz/30 g roasted almonds, chopped

½ teaspoon dried chilli flakes, (optional)

Sea salt flakes

Method

Preheat oven to 180°C/350°F/Gas mark 4.

Place the beetroot onto a sheet of foil and drizzle with ¾ fl oz/20 ml of the oil and season with sea salt. Seal the foil around the beetroot and place onto an oven tray.

Coat the pumpkin with ¾ fl oz/20 ml of the oil and season with sea salt. Place the pumpkin and beetroot onto a large oven tray and bake for 20 minutes.

Coat the carrots, onion, broccoli and mushroom with 1¾ fl oz/40 ml of the oil and place onto another tray. Bake with the beetroot and pumpkin and continue to cook for another 25–30 minutes, or until the vegetables are golden and cooked through. Remove the beetroot from the foil when once cool enough to handle, remove the skin and slice in half.

Meanwhile, coat the chicken in the remaining oil, cumin, cinnamon and a pinch of sea salt. Heat a non-stick frying pan over a medium heat and cook the chicken for 2–3 minutes each side, or until cooked through and fragrant. Rest the chicken for 3–4 minutes before slicing into strips.

To serve, arrange all vegetables onto a large serving board. Scatter over the sliced chicken and tahini yogurt. Squeeze over the lemon and top with the almonds and dried chilli. Serve warm.

Tandoori Chicken Salad with Spiced Yogurt & Mango Chutney

Serves 2

A fresh and light recipe to get an Indian spice fix! This dish is a veritable flavour-bomb. Chicken cooked on the bone always yields a succulent result, but if you're short on time, feel free to grill chicken breast or thigh, which has been marinated in the Tandoori mix for a speedier version.

Ingredients

2¼ lb/1 kg whole free-range chicken
1 tablespoon tandoori paste
⅓ cup Greek (strained plain) yogurt
1 small red onion, thinly sliced
1 lime
3 oz/80 g mixed salad leaves
1 Lebanese cucumber, sliced
1 tomato, cut into wedges
1 small carrot, sliced into ribbons using a vegetable peeler
1 long red chilli, sliced
½ cup/4 tablespoons mint, leaves picked
½ cup/4 tablespoons coriander (cilantro), leaves picked
2 tablespoons mango chutney

For the Spiced Yogurt:

1 cup/8 oz/250 g Greek (strained plain) yogurt
1 teaspoon ground cumin seeds
1 teaspoon garam masala
2 teaspoons honey
Sea salt flakes

Method

Preheat the oven to 180°C/350°F/Gas mark 4.

Pat the chicken dry using kitchen paper and place into a large bowl. Mix together the yogurt, tandoori paste and a good pinch of sea salt and rub the mixture all over the chicken. Place the chicken onto a lined oven tray and roast for 55-60 minutes, or until golden and cooked through. Remove the chicken from the oven and allow to rest for 10 minutes before slicing into quarters.

Meanwhile, to make the spiced yogurt, place the cumin and garam masala into a small non-stick frying pan set over a medium heat. Dry toast the spices for 1 minute, or until just fragrant. Whisk the spices into the yogurt with honey and a small pinch of salt. Set aside in the refrigerator.

Place the sliced onion into a bowl and squeeze over the juice of half a lime, a pinch of sea salt and leave for 10 minutes to take the raw edge from the onion.

To serve, place the salad leaves, cucumber, tomato, carrot, chilli, mint and coriander into serving bowls. Drizzle over half of the spiced yogurt and place on the roast chicken. Top with the mango chutney, onions, remaining yogurt and lime wedges.

Note
Tandoori paste and mango chutney can be found in most supermarkets with the Indian foods, or condiments.

French Lentil &
Poached Chicken Salad

Serves 4

The French lentils give this dish a great 'pop' and the tangy mustard dressing ties it all together perfectly.

Ingredients

2 x 7 oz/200 g skinless chicken breast, trimmed

1¾ pints/1 litre chicken stock

4 bay leaves

6 peppercorns

2 garlic cloves, skin on, cut in half

1 brown onion, skin on, cut in quarters

9 oz/250 g green or yellow French (green) beans, trimmed and halved lengthways

5 oz/150 g French puy lentils, washed

4 free-range eggs

2 cups/4 oz/115 g lettuce (butter or cos/Romaine), washed and torn

¼ cup/2 tablespoons chives, finely chopped

¼ cup/2 tablespoons tarragon leaves, torn

⅓ cup/2½ tablespoons flat leaf parsley, chopped

Sea salt flakes and ground pepper

For the Dressing:

2 fl oz/60 ml olive oil

1 tablespoon Dijon mustard

1 fl oz/30 ml white wine vinegar

1 tablespoon honey

Method

To poach the chicken, pour the stock into a large saucepan and add the bay leaves, peppercorns, garlic and onion. Bring to the boil, then reduce the heat to a very gentle simmer and add the chicken. Cover with a lid and poach over very low heat for 10 minutes.

Remove the pan from the heat and leave the chicken poaching in the stock for another 20–25 minutes to cook through. Remove the chicken from the stock and set aside.

Discard the peppercorns, bay leaves, garlic and onion and return the stock to the heat and bring to a boil. Add the green beans and blanch for 1–2 minutes, then remove with a slotted spoon and set aside. Add the lentils, cover and cook for 20 minutes, or until tender and cooked through. Drain and set aside.

Put the eggs in pan of salted water and bring to the boil. Boil for 6–8 minutes, remove from the heat and cool immediately in a bowl of chilled water. Peel and discard the shells and set aside.

For the dressing, whisk all the ingredients together and season with sea salt and a pinch of ground white pepper.

Roughly tear the chicken into strips and place into a bowl with the green beans, lentils, lettuce, chives, tarragon and parsley and pour over the dressing. Toss well to combine and divide between serving bowls. Slice the eggs and scatter over the top of the salad, then drizzle with a little extra olive oil.

Five Spice Chicken & Crispy Noodle Salad

Serves 4

If you like textures and flavours that are crispy, crunchy, fragrant and tangy, this recipe has it all.

Ingredients

2 teaspoons Chinese five spice
  powder
2 tablespoons olive oil
4 x 6 oz/180 g chicken breasts,
  skin on
2 Lebanese cucumbers
2 green spring onions
  (scallions), finely sliced
3 cups/9 oz/270 g Chinese
  cabbage (wombok), finely
  sliced
3½ oz/100 g Asian fried egg
  noodles
½ cup/4 tablespoons coriander
  (cilantro) leaves, torn
3 oz/80 g roasted unsalted
  cashews
Sea salt flakes and pepper

For the Dressing:

2 teaspoons sesame oil
1 tablespoon Asian sesame
  paste

2 teaspoons ginger, grated
1 fl oz/30 ml soy sauce
1 tablespoon caster (superfine) sugar
1 tablespoon rice vinegar
1 long red chilli, seeded, finely chopped

Method

Heat a non-stick frying pan over a medium heat. Mix together the 5 spice powder, olive oil and a pinch of sea salt in a bowl and toss with the chicken to coat.

Cook the chicken for 3–4 minutes each side, or until golden and cooked through. Remove from the heat and allow to rest for 5 minutes before slicing each breast into ¼ in/0.5 cm thick slices.

Meanwhile, slice the cucumbers into ribbons using a vegetable peeler, working around the seed core. Put into a bowl and toss with the spring onions, cabbage, egg noodles and half the coriander.

Divide the noodle salad into serving bowls.

In a bowl, whisk together all the dressing ingredients until well combined. Place the sliced chicken breast on top of the salads and scatter over the remaining coriander and cashew nuts. Drizzle over the dressing and serve.

Smoked Chicken Cobb Salad with Blue Cheese Dressing

Serves 4

This American-inspired garden salad combines salty bacon, smoked chicken and sweetcorn kernels all wrapped up in a creamy blue cheese dressing.

Ingredients

20 cherry tomatoes, halved

Olive oil, to drizzle

4 free-range eggs

2 cobs corn

4 rashers (strips) smoked middle bacon, rind removed

10½ oz/300 g whole smoked chicken breast, sliced

2 cups/4 oz/115 g gem lettuce, washed and sliced

½ cup/3 oz/85 g inner celery leaves, for garnish

Sea salt flakes

For the Blue Cheese Dressing:

½ cup/4 fl oz/125 ml buttermilk

2 tablespoons quality mayonnaise

1 tablespoon chives, finely sliced, plus extra to serve

3 oz/80 g Roquefort cheese, or any good quality blue cheese

2 teaspoons maple syrup

Method

Preheat the oven to 160°C/325°F/Gas mark 3. Place the tomatoes skin side down on a lined oven tray and drizzle with a little olive oil and sea salt flakes. Roast the tomatoes for 20–25, or until semi dried and slightly wrinkled. Set aside.

Meanwhile, put the eggs in a pan of salted water and bring to the boil. Reduce the heat to a simmer and boil for 6–8 minutes. Remove from the heat and place in a bowl of chilled water. Once cool enough to handle, peel, slice and set aside.

Boil the corn in salted water for 4–5 minutes. Remove from the heat and once cool enough to handle, slice the kernels from the cob.

Heat a non-stick frying pan over medium heat and fry the bacon for 2–3 minutes each side, or until crispy. Remove from the heat and set aside.

Place all the dressing ingredients into the bowl of a small food processor and blend until smooth. Check for seasoning and adjust as necessary.

Arrange the lettuce, smoked chicken, tomatoes, eggs, corn, bacon and celery leaves on a serving plate. Drizzle over the dressing, scatter over extra chives and serve.

Note: Smoked chicken breast can be found in specialty food stores. You could use BBQ chicken or grilled chicken breast instead.

Smoked Chicken, Kale & Celeriac
with Lemon Caesar Dressing

Serves 4

I've taken all the good bits of a classic Caesar salad and twisted them into a modern delight with this recipe. Smoked chicken, fresh pear, crunchy celery and earthy kale make for a quirky version. Once I discovered how delicious and nutritious kale can be raw, I started to incorporate it into a lot of my salads... Hail kale!

Ingredients

7 oz/200 g middle bacon, rind removed

1 tablespoon olive oil

2 thick slices sourdough bread, crust removed

12½ oz/350 g whole smoked chicken breast, sliced into ⅛ in/0.5 cm strips

3 cups/1 lb 450 g celeriac, peeled, sliced into matchsticks

2 stalks celery, finely sliced

4 kale stems, stalks removed, leaves finely sliced

1 green pear, core removed, thinly sliced

3½ oz/100 g Parmesan, shaved

Sea salt flakes

For the Dressing:

½ garlic clove, finely grated

½ cup/4 fl oz/125 ml buttermilk

2 tablespoons quality mayonnaise

1 tablespoon lemon juice

2 teaspoons finely grated lemon zest

1 tablespoon maple syrup

2 teaspoons Dijon mustard

1 anchovy fillet, drained and finely chopped

Method

Heat a non-stick frying pan over a medium-high heat. Add the bacon and cook for 2–3 minutes each side, or until golden and crisp. Remove from the heat and set aside to drain on paper towel and cool.

Return the pan to a medium heat and add the olive oil. Place the sourdough bread into the bowl of a small food processor and blitz to crumbs. Tip the breadcrumbs into the pan and fry, stirring, for 4–5 minutes, or until golden and crisp. Season with a pinch of sea salt, take off the heat and set aside.

In a small bowl, whisk together all the dressing ingredients until smooth.

In a large bowl, combine the sliced chicken, celeriac, celery, kale, pear and Parmesan. Pour over the dressing and toss well to coat. Arrange the salad on serving platters, break over pieces of the bacon and scatter over the breadcrumbs.

Notes
Celeriac oxidizes easily when cut, so put the cut pieces it into a bowl of cold water with a squeeze of lemon added to stop them from turning brown.
Smoked chicken breast can be found at specialty food stores. You could use grilled chicken breast instead.

Duck & Orange Couscous Salad with Fresh Cherries

Serves 4

This is a wonderful festive dish to serve around Easter or Christmas. If you can't find fresh cherries, try substituting with a jar of morello cherries, sour-dried cherries or cranberries.

Ingredients

4 duck breasts

2 teaspoons ground cumin

1 teaspoon ground cinnamon

1 cup/6 oz/175 g wholewheat couscous

¾ oz/20 g butter

1 large orange, segmented

20 fresh cherries, washed and pits removed

½ cup/4 tablespoons flat leaf parsley, chopped

¼ cup/2 tablespoons chives, finely sliced

⅓ cup/1½ oz/40 g toasted pistachio nuts, chopped

Micro red cress, to garnish

Sea salt flakes and black pepper

For the Dressing:

¼ cup/2 fl oz/60ml fresh orange juice

2 teaspoons finely grated orange zest

1 fl oz/30 ml lemon juice

1 tablespoon honey

1 teaspoon Dijon mustard

1¾ fl oz/50 ml olive oil

Method

Preheat the oven to 180°C/350°F/Gas mark 4.

Using a sharp knife, lightly score the skin of the duck breast then coat in the cumin, cinnamon and season with sea salt and pepper. Place the duck skin-side down in a cold ovenproof pan and set over medium heat. Fry the duck for 8–10 minutes, or until most of the fat has rendered out of the skin and it is golden. Turn the duck over, place into the oven and cook for another 5 minutes. Remove the duck from the oven, place onto a warm plate, cover with foil and leave to rest for 10 minutes before slicing into generous ⅛ in/0.5 cm strips.

Meanwhile, place the couscous into a large bowl. Mix together ¾ cup/6 fl oz/175 ml of boiling water with the butter, and stir until the butter has melted and pour over the couscous. Stir until most of the water has been soaked up then cover with plastic wrap and leave to soak for 5 minutes. Remove the plastic wrap and using a fork, gently stir the couscous to separate the grains.

Whisk together all the dressing ingredients along with a pinch of sea salt and pepper then pour over the couscous. Add in the parsley and chives then stir well to combine. Divide the couscous onto serving bowls and top with the orange segments and cherries. Place over the sliced duck and garnish with pistachio nuts and micro cress.

Balinese Chicken, Charred Corn & Papaya Salad

Serves 4

I've travelled to Bali numerous times and despite the cuisine being renowned for being so varied and interesting, one of my favourite things to eat while holidaying is the sweet red papaya and fresh lime they often serve during breakfast. That combination in this salad takes me back to Bali.

Ingredients

2 x 7 oz/200g chicken breasts, trimmed

1 garlic clove, crushed

1 tablespoon ginger, grated

1 tablespoon lemongrass, grated

2 teaspoons ground coriander

1 teaspoon turmeric

1 teaspoon brown sugar

2 fl oz/60 ml olive oil

3 cobs corn, husk removed

10½ oz/300 g snake beans or French (green) beans, sliced into 2 in/5 cm lengths

1 ripe avocado, peeled and chopped

2 cups red papaya, peeled and sliced

1½ fl oz/40 ml fresh lime juice

½ bunch/4 tablespoons coriander (cilantro), leaves picked

½ cup/2 oz/60 g roasted peanuts, chopped

Lime wedges, to serve

Sea salt flakes

Method

Place the chicken into a large bowl along with the garlic, ginger, lemongrass, ground coriander, turmeric, brown sugar and half of the oil. Toss well to coat the chicken, then set aside to marinate for 30 minutes.

Meanwhile, heat a non-stick frying pan set over a medium/high heat and place the corn cobs into the pan and cook, turning for 10–12 minutes, or until the corn has some dark brown char marks on the outside. Allow the corn to cool before slicing the kernels off the cob and place them into a large bowl.

Heat the remaining oil in the same pan and cook the beans over a medium heat with a pinch of sea salt for 3–4 minutes, or until just tender. Remove the beans from the pan and toss in the bowl with the corn.

Heat a non-stick pan over a medium heat and cook the chicken for 3–4 minutes each side, or until cooked through and fragrant. Allow the chicken to rest for 5 minutes before slicing.

To serve, place the corn and bean mixture onto serving bowls. Scatter over the avocado and papaya and drizzle with the lime juice. Arrange the chicken on top of the salad and garnish with coriander, peanuts and lime wedges.

Black Pepper & Lemongrass Chicken Salad

Serves 4

This fragrant and textural salad is great to serve as a starter! The crispy iceberg lettuce and fresh herbs ensure it's nice and light with plenty of room for mains!

Ingredients

1 lb 2 oz/500 g organic chicken thighs, trimmed

1 tablespoon sunflower oil

2 teaspoons fresh ground black pepper

1 teaspoon dried chilli flakes

2 kaffir lime leaves, very finely sliced

2 teaspoons lemongrass, finely grated

2 teaspoons fresh ginger, finely grated

1 red chilli, seeded and finely chopped

1 tablespoon brown sugar

2 teaspoons sesame oil

1 fl oz/30 ml fish sauce (nam pla)

1 fl oz/30 ml fresh lime juice

2 cups/4 oz/115 g iceberg lettuce, finely sliced

2 cups/6 oz/150 g Chinese cabbage, finely sliced

1 Lebanese cucumber, seeded and finely sliced

¼ cup/2 tablespoons coriander, thinly shredded

¼ cup2 tablespoons mint leaves, finely shredded

¼ cup/1 oz/30 g roasted peanuts, chopped

Sea salt flakes

Method

Preheat the grill (broiler) to high and line a grill tray with kitchen foil.

Butterfly-cut the chicken thighs so they are about ¾ in/1.5 cm thick.

Combine the sunflower oil, pepper, chilli flakes and a small pinch of sea salt. Brush over the chicken, then place the chicken onto the grill tray and cook for 10–12 minutes, or until golden and cooked through. Remove the chicken from the heat and set aside to cool slightly.

Meanwhile, place the kaffir lime, lemongrass, ginger, chilli, sugar, sesame oil, fish sauce and lime in a large bowl.

Once the chicken is cool enough to handle, use a large sharp knife to finely chop the chicken into rough mince. Do not blend in a food processor. Add the warm chicken to the bowl with the dressing ingredients and toss well. Mix in the lettuce, cabbage, cucumber, coriander, mint and gently combine. Divide the salad between the serving bowls and top with roasted peanuts and extra chilli flakes. Serve warm.

Duck Salad with Pickled Daikon & Sesame Dressing

Serves 4

This is a great exotic salad to try. The pickled daikon and fresh pear work really well with the rich duck meat.

Ingredients

4 duck breasts

5 oz/150 g piece daikon, peeled and then sliced into julienne strips

1 tablespoon rice vinegar

1 tablespoon caster (superfine) sugar

1 teaspoon sea salt

1 bunch asparagus, trimmed

1 ripe pear, washed

2¾ oz/80 g mizuna or baby endive leaves

1 tablespoon chives, finely sliced

2 teaspoons nanami togarashi (Japanese seven spice chilli mix), optional

Sea salt flakes and pepper

For the Sesame Dressing:

1 tablespoon tahini paste

2 teaspoons sesame oil

1 tablespoon mirin

1 tablespoon soy sauce

1 tablespoon caster (superfine) sugar

2 tablespoons rice vinegar

Method

Preheat the oven to 180°C/350°F/Gas mark 4.

Lightly score the duck skin, then season the flesh with sea salt and pepper. Place the duck, skin-side down, in a cold, ovenproof frying pan, then fry over medium heat for 8–10 minutes, or until most of the fat has rendered and the skin is golden and crisp. Turn the duck over, then transfer the pan to the oven and cook for 5 minutes for medium, or until cooked to your liking. Transfer to a plate, cover loosely with foil and rest for 5 minutes, before slicing into generous ⅛ in/0.5 cm strips.

Meanwhile, place the rice vinegar, sugar and salt into a bowl at stir to dissolve. Add in the daikon, cover and leave to pickle for 20 minutes. Drain and discard the liquid.

Cook the asparagus in a saucepan of boiling salted water for 2 minutes. Drain, then refresh under running cold water, then cut in half lengthways. Set aside.

To make the dressing, whisk together all ingredients in a bowl until smooth.

Remove the core from the pear and using a mandolin or sharp knife, thinly slice the pear and mix together in a large bowl with the mizuna, pickled daikon, and asparagus and toss salad gently to combine.

Divide the salad between the serving bowls or plates then top with duck and drizzle with sesame dressing, chives and spice mix, if using.

Notes

Togarashi Japanese spice mix is available at Asian supermarkets. Substitute the spice mix with black or white sesame seeds, if you prefer.

Chinese Duck & Lychee Salad

Serves 4

Duck meat always works well with something sweet. I love to use lychees in this salad. Fresh plum, pear and green apple are all very good alternatives if you can't get your hands on any lychees.

Ingredients

½ Chinese roast duck*, meat shredded

16 lychees, peeled, halved and seeded

2 golden shallots, peeled and finely sliced

1 bunch watercress, washed, sprigs picked

1 Lebanese cucumber, seeded and sliced

1 cup/2½ oz/75 g coriander (cilantro), leaves picked

2 tablespoons roasted unsalted peanuts

2 tablespoons Asian fried golden shallots

For the Dressing:

1 tablespoon hoisin sauce

1 tablespoon rice wine vinegar

2 teaspoons brown sugar

1 small knob ginger, finely grated

2 teaspoons sesame oil

2 teaspoons sesame seeds, toasted

Method

Whisk together all the dressing ingredients in a bowl and set aside.

Combine the shredded duck, lychees, golden shallots, watercress, cucumber and coriander leaves in a large bowl. Divide the salad between serving bowls. Drizzle over the dressing and scatter with peanuts and fried golden shallots.

Note
Asian fried golden shallots can be found in the Asian section of supermarkets.
*Chinese roast duck can be found in Asian BBQ shops.

Lamb

Spiced Lamb &
Hummus Salad Bowl

Serves 4

Apart from looking spectacular, this recipe is graced with some beautiful Lebanese / Middle Eastern flavours. It's really designed for sharing, so gather your friends, break some bread and get in early before it's all gone!

Ingredients

2 x 7 oz/200 g lamb backstrap/loin, trimmed

1 tablespoon ground cumin

1 teaspoon ground cinnamon

1¾ fl oz/50 ml olive oil

2 small red onions, finely sliced

1¼ fl oz/40 ml red wine vinegar

1 tablespoon caster (superfine) sugar

1 x 14 oz/400 g can chickpeas, drained

1 Lebanese cucumber, seeded and sliced

5 oz/150 g cherry tomatoes, halved

½ cup/4 tablespoons flat leaf parsley, chopped

½ cup/4 tablespoons mint, chopped

3 cups lemon hummus (see page 18)

½ cup/3 oz/85 g green olives

½ cup/3 oz/85 g pomegranate seeds

1 cup/8 oz/250 g Greek (strained plain) yogurt

2 teaspoons ground sweet paprika

Warm flatbread or sourdough to serve

Sea salt flakes and black pepper

Method

Coat the lamb with the ground cumin and cinnamon. Season with sea salt then set aside to marinate at room temperature for 20 minutes.

Meanwhile, place the sliced onion into a non-metallic bowl and sprinkle with 1 teaspoon of sea salt. Add in the red wine vinegar and sugar and stir to dissolve. Leave the onion to lightly pickle for 20–30 minutes before draining. Set aside.

Heat ¾ fl oz/20 ml of the olive oil in a non-stick frying pan set over a medium heat. Cook the lamb for 3–4 minutes each side for medium. Remove the lamb from the pan and set aside in a warm area to rest for 5 minutes before slicing into thin strips.

In a large bowl combine the chickpeas, cucumber, tomato, parsley and mint and season with sea salt and pepper.

To serve, line a serving bowl or wooden board with the lemon hummus, using the back of a spoon to spread it out. Arrange the lamb on top of the hummus along with the chickpea salad, pickled onion and olives. Add a dollop of yogurt and scatter with pomegranate seeds. Drizzle over the remaining olive oil and sweet paprika. Serve with warm breads.

Butterflied Lamb, Sweet Potato & Pearl Couscous Salad

Serves 6

This dish is great for a shared lunch table or casual dinner. Serve it on a large platter or wooden board in the centre of the table.

Ingredients

1.5 k/3 lb 5 oz butterflied leg of lamb

1 tablespoon sweet paprika

1 tablespoon whole cumin seeds

1 tablespoon coriander seeds, lightly crushed

3½ fl oz/100 ml olive oil

800 g/1¾ lb red sweet potato, (kumera) skin washed, cut into wedges lengthways

1 teaspoon ground cinnamon

2 red onions, cut into wedges

10½ oz/300 g pearl couscous

1 cup/8 fl oz/250 ml tahini yogurt (see page 16)

½ cup/2 oz/60 g pistachio nuts, toasted and chopped

1 cup/2½ oz/75 g coriander (cilantro), chopped

½ cup/1¼ oz/40 g mint, leaves picked

½ cup/3 oz/85 g fresh pomegranate seeds

¼ cup/2 fl oz/60 ml lemon juice

1 tablespoon honey

1 teaspoon ground cumin

Sea salt flakes and black pepper

Method

Preheat the oven to 180°C/350°F/Gas mark 4.

Remove the lamb from the refrigerator 1 hour before cooking.

Combine the paprika, cumin seeds, coriander seeds and ¾ fl oz/20 ml of olive oil in a small bowl. Spoon the paprika mixture over the lamb, season with sea salt and black pepper and rub in using clean hands.

Place the sweet potato and onion into a large bowl and coat with 1 fl oz/30 ml of the olive oil, cinnamon and a pinch of sea salt. Place onto a lined oven tray.

Heat a large non-stick frying pan over a medium-high heat, add the lamb and brown on both sides for 2–3 minutes. Transfer the lamb into a roasting tray and bake in the oven along with the sweet potato and onions for 25–30 minutes for medium, or a little longer depending on your preference.

Remove the lamb from the oven, cover with foil to keep warm and set aside to rest for 15 minutes before slicing into strips across the grain.

Leave the sweet potato and onion in the oven cooking for 10–15 minutes longer while the lamb is resting then remove, keep warm and set aside.

Meanwhile, cook the couscous in a saucepan of boiling salted water for 8 minutes, or until tender. Rinse under cold running water, then drain well.

To make the dressing, toast the ground cumin in a small frying pan over low heat. Cook for 1 minute, or until fragrant then remove from the heat and whisk together with the lemon juice, honey, remaining oil and season with a pinch of sea salt.

Toss the couscous with the dressing and pour onto a large serving platter. Top with the sliced lamb and scatter over roasted sweet potato, onions, tahini yogurt, pistachio nuts, coriander, mint and pomegranate seeds. Serve warm.

Slow Roast Lamb Shoulder, Cauliflower & Pistachio Salad

Serves 4–6

Is there anything more tantalising than the aroma of lamb slowly cooking? Once cooked, the meat practically falls off the bone. The creamy cauliflower and spicy yogurt are the perfect partners for the lamb.

Ingredients

For the Slow-Braised Lamb Shoulder:

1 lamb shoulder on the bone, about 1.8–2 kg/4–4 1/1 lbs
2 teaspoons whole cumin seeds
2 teaspoons whole coriander seeds
2 teaspoons whole fennel seeds
2 teaspoons sea salt
1 teaspoon cracked black pepper
2 tablespoons olive oil

For the Lemon Harissa Yogurt:

1½ cups (12 fl oz/375 ml) plain Greek (strained plain) yogurt
2 teaspoons lemon zest, finely grated
2 tablespoons lemon juice
1 tablespoon harissa paste
1 tablespoon honey

1 head cauliflower, trimmed and sliced into florets
1¼ fl oz/40 ml olive oil
1 cup/2½ oz/75 g mint leaves, torn
⅓ cup/2½ oz/75 g dried cranberries
2 oz/60 g pistachio nuts, roughly chopped

Method

Remove the lamb from the refrigerator 1 hour prior to cooking to bring to room temperature and trim off any excess fat from the edges of the shoulder.

Toast the cumin, coriander and fennel seeds in a small pan over a medium heat for 1 minute, or until fragrant. Place the toasted seeds into a mortar and pestle along with the salt and pepper. Grind into a powder, mix with the oil and rub all over the lamb.

Preheat the oven to 170°C/340°F/Gas mark 3½. Place the lamb into a roasting tray along with ½ cup/4 fl oz/125 ml of water. Cover the tray with foil and roast the lamb for 4 hours. Remove the foil from the lamb and cook uncovered for another 20 minutes, or until the lamb is golden and the meat can easily be pulled from the bone. Remove from the oven and allow lamb to rest for 15 minutes before using two forks to shred the meat from the bone. Keep warm.

While the lamb is cooking, toss the cauliflower with the olive oil and a pinch of sea salt in a bowl. Place the cauliflower onto a lined baking tray and roast in the oven with the lamb for 35–40 minutes, or until golden and tender. Remove the cauliflower from the oven and set aside. Mix together all the ingredients for the yogurt dressing in a bowl until well combined.

To serve, put the cauliflower and half of the mint onto a serving platter. Drizzle over half of the yogurt dressing and arrange the lamb on top. Dress the lamb with the remaining yogurt, remaining mint leaves, cranberries and pistachio nuts. Serve warm with extra lemon wedges.

Note:
Harissa is a hot pepper paste from North Africa. It can be found in specialty food stores and delis.

Spiced Lamb & Charred Capsicum Salad with Mint Yogurt Dressing

Serves 6–8

It's really hard for me to pick favourties in this book, but if I had to then this dish would be close to the top of my list.

Ingredients

For the Spiced Roast Lamb:

1 tablespoon whole peppercorns

1 tablespoon coriander seeds, toasted

1 tablespoon whole cumin seeds, toasted

2 tablespoons olive oil

1 tablespoon sea salt flakes

2 garlic cloves, peeled

2 teaspoons ground cardamom

2 kg/4½ lb lamb leg, with bone in

For the Mint Yogurt Dressing:

1 cup/8 fl oz/250 ml Greek (strained plain) yogurt

⅔ cup/5 fl oz/160 g good quality mayonnaise

¼ cup/2 tablespoons mint, finely chopped, plus extra whole leave

¼ cup/2 tablespoons coriander (cilantro), finely chopped

½ teaspoon sea salt

3 large red capsicum (bell peppers), washed

9 oz/250 g baby rocket (arugula) leaves

7 oz/200 g cherry tomatoes, halved

3½ oz/100 g good quality crumbly feta cheese

Method

Preheat the oven to 180°C/350°F/Gas mark 4.

Place the peppercorns, coriander seeds and cumin seeds in a mortar and pestle or the bowl of a small food processor. Grind the seeds to a rough powder then add the oil, salt, garlic and cardamom. Mix to form a smooth paste. Rub the paste all over the lamb leg and place the meat into a baking tray. Set aside at room temperature for 1 hour to marinate, then bake in the oven for 1½–2 hours. Remove the lamb from the oven, cover and allow to rest for 15 minutes before slicing. Set aside and keep warm.

Meanwhile, put the whole capsicum on the grill (broiler) pan. Turn the grill (broiler) to high and cook the capsicum, turning occasionally for 8–10 minutes, until the skin has blackened and is blistered. Set aside to cool, then remove and discard the skin, seeds and membrane. Slice the flesh into ½ in/1 cm strips.

Mix all the yogurt dressing ingredients together in a bowl.

Arrange the rocket in the base of a large serving platter or bowl along with the tomatoes, capsicum and feta cheese. Place the sliced lamb onto the salad, making sure to add any spice mix that may have fallen off while slicing. Drizzle over the yogurt dressing and scatter with extra mint leaves. Serve warm.

Egg Net with Red Curry Lamb & Bean Sprout Salad

Serves 4

Curry can sometimes be a heavy dish, but I've taken the best elements out of a curry and made it into a lighter and much fresher Asian-Styled salad

Ingredients

4 small free-range eggs, beaten

2 fl oz/60 ml sunflower oil

1 lb 6 oz/600 g lamb backstrap (loin) fillet, trimmed

1 tablespoon Thai red curry paste

14 fl oz/400 ml coconut milk

1 tablespoon fish sauce (nam pla)

1 tablespoon brown sugar

¾ fl oz/25 ml lime juice

1 green shallot, thinly sliced

1 Lebanese cucumber, seeded and thinly sliced

7 oz/200 g bean sprouts

1 long red chilli, seeded and sliced

1 cup/2½ oz/75 g Thai basil leaves

1 cup/2½ oz/75 g coriander (cilantro) leaves

1 cup/2½ oz/75 g mint leaves

¼ cup/1 oz/30 g roasted peanuts, roughly chopped

1 cup fresh coconut relish (see page 27), optional

Sea salt flakes and black pepper

Method

Strain the eggs through a sieve into a bowl and leave to settle for 1 hour. This allows the proteins in the egg to break down. Set aside.

Season the lamb and coat with ¾ fl oz/20 ml of the oil. Place in a non-stick frying pan set over medium heat and fry for 3–4 minutes on each side, or until cooked to your liking. Remove the lamb from the heat and set aside to rest. Slice into generous ⅛ in/0.5 cm strips.

Meanwhile, heat ¾ fl oz/20 ml of oil in a small saucepan, add the curry paste and cook for 1 minute. Pour in the coconut milk and bring to a simmer. Reduce the heat and cook for 5 minutes, or until slightly thickened. Remove from the heat and add the fish sauce, sugar and lime. Check for balance and set aside.

In a large bowl, combine the green shallot, cucumber, bean sprouts, chilli, Thai basil, coriander, and mint. Set aside.

For the egg net, heat a non-stick fry pan over a medium heat. Brush with a small amount of remaining oil. Dip your fingers into egg mixture and drizzle over the pan to form a cross-hatch pattern. Once the egg has set, remove it from the pan and repeat with remaining egg. You should have 4 large or 8 small egg nets.

Place the lamb into the salad mixture, pour over the dressing and mix well.

To serve, place the egg nets onto the base of serving bowls. Divide the salad on top of the egg nets and scatter over the peanuts. Fold the egg net over the salad to form a pocket and top with the fresh coconut relish. Garnish with extra lime wedges.

Pork

Creamy Celeriac Salad with Jamon & Manchego Cheese

Serves 4

This is a really delicious dish. It's relatively easy to make, because there's no cooking involved and the celeriac gives great crunch to counteract the creamy dressing. Manchego cheese and jamon are two classic Spanish ingredients that work a treat together. Both can be found in specialty delicatessens.

Ingredients

1 medium celeriac bulb

1 lemon

12 thin slices jamon, torn

2¾ oz/80 g Manchego cheese, shaved

2 green spring onions (scallions), finely sliced

¼ cup/2 tablespoons flat leaf parsley, finely sliced

⅔ cup (5½ fl oz/165 g) Greek (strained plain) yogurt

⅓ cup/2½ oz/75 g quality mayonnaise

1 tablespoon honey

Sea salt flakes and ground white and black peppers

Method

Peel and slice the celeriac into thin matchsticks. Place the sliced celeriac into a large bowl of chilled water and squeeze in the lemon juice. This will prevent the celeriac from turning brown while you prepare the rest of the ingredients.

Mix together the yogurt, mayonnaise and honey and season with a pinch of sea salt and ground white pepper.

Drain the celeriac from the lemon water and pat dry on a clean kitchen towel. Toss the celeriac with the yogurt dressing and half of the spring onions and parsley.

Divide the celeriac between serving bowls or plates and add the jamon and shaved Manchego cheese. Scatter with the remaining spring onion, parsley and a grind of cracked black pepper.

Vietnamese Pork
& Fresh Herb Salad

Serves 4–6

Vietnamese food is all about simple and vibrant ingredients. There are lots of fresh herbs and a good balance of sweet, sour, salty and hot... All the things I love about food.

Ingredients

14 oz/400 g piece pork fillet, trimmed and cut into ¼ in/0.5 cm thick slices

2 tablespoons vegetable oil

For the Marinade:

1 tablespoon fresh ginger, finely sliced

2 garlic cloves, crushed

1 tablespoon fish sauce (nam pla)

1 tablespoon honey

½ teaspoon black pepper

1 teaspoon sesame oil

For the Noodle Salad:

5 oz/150 g thin rice vermicelli noodles

2 cups Chinese cabbage (wombok), thinly sliced

1 long red chilli, finely chopped

½ cup/1¼ oz/40 g Vietnamese mint, chopped (use regular mint if Vietnamese mint is not available)

½ cup/1¼ oz/40 g fresh coriander (cilantro), torn

½ cup/1¼ oz/40 g perilla leaves (use Thai basil if perilla is not available)

1 cucumber, deseeded, finely sliced

2 tablespoons roast peanuts, roughly chopped

For the Dressing:

½ cup (4 fl oz/125 ml) white vinegar

½ cup (3½ oz/100 g) caster (superfine) sugar

2 teaspoons fish sauce (nam pla)

1 teaspoon chilli oil

½ teaspoon sesame oil

Juice of 1 lime, or to taste

Method

Put the pork into a bowl, cover with the marinade ingredients and set aside for 15 minutes.

Put the noodles in a large bowl, cover with hot water and stand for 5 minutes, or until soft. Cut the noodles a few times with scissors to about 4 in/10 cm long, drain and set aside to cool.

For the dressing, place the vinegar, sugar and ¼ cup/2 fl oz/ 60 ml of water into a small saucepan. Place over a medium heat. Stir until the sugar has dissolved. Simmer for 6–8 minutes, or until reduced by half. Add the fish sauce, chilli oil, sesame oil and lime. Set aside.

Heat the oil in a non-stick frying pan set over a high heat. Cook the pork in few batches for 3–4 minutes, or until sticky and golden.

Place the noodles, lettuce, red chilli, mint, coriander, perilla leaves, cucumber and half the pork in a large bowl. Pour over the dressing and toss to coat. Place the noodle salad onto a serving platter. Scatter over the remaining pork and garnish with peanuts, extra herbs and a lime wedge.

Pork & Shrimp Dumpling Salad with Ginger Dressing

Serves 4

I've been making these dumplings for years. You can make a big batch and freeze them in advance. They're great served as a canapé or in an aromatic broth when the weather's a little cooler.

Ingredients

24 won ton egg pastry wrappers

1 egg, for brushing, beaten

3 cups baby spinach leaves

2 cups snow peas, blanched and finely sliced lengthways

2 cups snow pea sprouts

For the Dumpling Filling:

9 oz/250 g (ground) pork mince

20 raw green shrimp, peeled and roughly chopped

1 tablespoon ginger, finely chopped

2 garlic cloves, crushed

1 tablespoon coriander (cilantro) stems, finely sliced

2 tablespoons green shallots, white part finely sliced, green part reserved for garnish

1 teaspoon sesame oil

½ teaspoon white pepper

1 teaspoon caster (superfine) sugar

1 tablespoon light soy sauce

For the Dressing:

¼ cup (2 fl oz/60 ml) peanut oil

1 tablespoon ginger, sliced into julienne strips

2 tablespoons light soy sauce

1 tablespoon Chinese black vinegar

1 teaspoon sesame oil

1 teaspoon caster sugar

Method

Place the dumpling filling ingredients in a bowl, and mix well.

Place the wonton wrappers on a clean tea towel. Place 1 level tablespoon of the dumpling mixture in the centre of the wrapper. Brush the outside of the wrapper with a little egg or water. Fold the dumpling over from corner to corner to form a triangle, ensuring that no air is inside. Place a little egg on one corner of the dumpling, and bring it around to meet the other side, (this will form a collar on the dumpling and allow the dressing to sit in the pocket). Repeat with all the dumplings.

Bring a large, wide pan of salted water to a gentle simmer. Slide the dumplings into the pan and gently poach for 5–7 minutes, occasionally moving around to ensure they do not stick.

Meanwhile, heat the peanut oil in a small saucepan until almost at smoking point. Place the ginger in a heat-proof bowl, and carefully pour over the hot oil. Leave to settle for 1 minute, then add the soy sauce, vinegar, sesame oil, sugar and mix well.

Remove the dumplings from the pan with a slotted spoon. Place the baby spinach, snow peas and snowpea shoots onto a serving plate. Top with the dumplings and drizzle with the dressing and scatter over reserved sliced green shallots.

Roast Pork, Apple & Cabbage Salad with Seeded Mustard Dressing

Serves 4

I've used pork belly in this recipe, but this would be the perfect dish to make with left-over roast pork. Chicken or turkey would also be very good in this salad... Christmas leftovers just got a new home!

Ingredients

750 g/1¾ lb boneless pork belly
2 tablespoons olive oil
1 teaspoon sea salt flakes
4 small green apples
4 cups/1¼ lb/600 g rocket (arugula) leaves
4 cups/8 oz/225 g savoy cabbage, finely shaved

For the Seeded Mustard Dressing:

1 tablespoon seeded mustard
1 fl oz/30 ml extra virgin olive oil
1 tablespoon quality mayonnaise
1 fl oz/30 ml white wine vinegar
1 tablespoon honey
Sea salt flakes and black pepper

Method

Preheat the oven to 180°C/350°F/Gas mark 4.

Peel and core the apples and slice them into quarters. Rub half of the oil into the apples and place them into a small lined roasting pan.

Score the pork skin and fat in a criss-cross pattern, without cutting into the meat. Rub the oil and salt into the pork, making sure to get some salt into the cut skin. Put the pork into an oven tray and roast along with the apples for 30 minutes, or until the apples are golden, but still holding their shape. Remove the apples from the oven and continue to cook the pork for another 30–40 minutes.

Increase the oven temperature to 200°C/400°F/Gas mark 6 and cook the pork for another 20 minutes, or until the pork is tender and the skin has crackled. Remove the pork from the oven and set aside to rest for 10–15 minutes before slicing into pieces.

Whisk together all the dressing ingredients along with a pinch of sea salt and black pepper until smooth. Place the rocket, cabbage, apples and pork into a large bowl. Pour the dressing over and gently toss well to coat. Divide the salad into bowls and serve immediately.

Green Papaya & Pork Salad with Sticky Chilli Lime Dressing

Serves 4

There are many variations you can make with this salad. You could add in shrimp, replace the pork with chicken and if you can't find green papaya, Lebanese cucumbers sliced into ribbons make a great and fresh alternative.

Ingredients

1 lb 6 oz/600 g Chinese crispy
  roast pork belly*, sliced
Asian fried shallots, to serve

For the Papaya Salad:

1 green papaya, about 1 lb/
  450 g, cut into julienne slices
1 Lebanese cucumber, seeds
  removed and finely sliced
2 long red chillies, seeds
  removed and finely sliced
2 golden shallots, finely sliced
1 cup/2½ oz/75 g Thai basil,
  leaves picked and washed
1 cup/2½ oz/75 g coriander
  (cilantro), leaves picked and
  washed
1 cup/2½ oz/75 g Vietnamese
  mint, leaves picked and
  washed

For the Sticky Chilli Lime Dressing:

2¾ fl oz/80 ml rice wine vinegar
1 fl oz/30 ml fish sauce (nam pla)
3 tablespoons caster (superfine) sugar
1 long red chilli, split in half
1 garlic clove, sliced
2 fl oz/60 ml lime juice

Method

For the sticky chilli lime dressing, combine the vinegar, fish sauce and sugar in a saucepan over a medium heat, stir to combine, add the chilli and garlic and bring to a simmer. Cook for 3–4 minutes, or until the mixture is slightly syrupy. Remove from heat, remove the chilli and cool to room temperature. Add the lime juice and set aside.

In a large bowl combine the papaya, cucumber, chilli, golden shallot and herbs, toss gently to combine, drizzle with dressing. Toss through the pork at the last minute and place into serving bowls. Scatter over fried shallots & serve.

Note
*Chinese crispy roast pork belly is from Chinese BBQ shops.

Lentil, Pea & Prosciutto Salad

Serves 4

This salad is best served as one of many sharing dishes. It`s a great 'Autumn Salad' and would pair very well with some crispy roast fish or chicken.

Ingredients

1 cup/8 oz/250 g black French (puy) lentils, washed

1½ cups/6 oz/175 g frozen baby peas, thawed

10 thin slices prosciutto

½ cup/1 ¼ oz/40 g flat leaf parsley, chopped

2 green spring onions (scallions), finely sliced

2 fl oz/60 ml olive oil

1 fl oz/30 ml white wine vinegar

1 tablespoon honey

1 teaspoon Dijon mustard

1 teaspoon sea salt flakes

½ teaspoon ground white pepper

Boil the lentils according to the packet instructions. Drain and set aside.

Cook the peas in boiling salted water for 2–3 minutes, drain and set aside.

Heat a non-stick frying pan over medium heat and cook the prosciutto for 2 minutes on each side, or until crispy.

Whisk together the oil, vinegar, honey, mustard, salt and pepper until well combined.

Toss the lentils, peas, parsley prosciutto and spring onions together in a bowl. Pour over the dressing, stir and place into serving bowls.

Prosciutto &
Yellow Peach Salad

Serves 4

I absolutely love a peach when in season! If you're looking for alternative ways to use peaches, give them a go in salads. They work really well here in this dish with peppery rocket leaves and salty prosciutto.

Ingredients

1¾ oz/50 ml extra virgin olive oil
1 fl oz/30 ml red wine vinegar
1 tablespoon maple syrup
120 g/4 oz baby rocket (arugula) leaves, washed
2 large yellow ripe peaches, sliced into thin wedges
20 thin slices prosciutto
⅓ cup/1½ oz/45 g slivered almonds, toasted
Sea salt flakes and ground black pepper

Method

Whisk together the oil, vinegar, maple syrup and a pinch of sea salt in a bowl.

Place the rocket into a large bowl and toss with half the dressing. Arrange the rocket, peaches and prosciutto on a serving platter. Drizzle with the remaining dressing, slivered almonds and cracked black pepper.

Fig, Savoury Ricotta & Prosciutto Salad

Serves 4

The fig season is short lived, so I like to make the most of this fruit when they're available. Figs are great used in breakfasts, desserts, salads or as part of a cheese board. I've combined these soft and sweet gems with creamy ricotta, bitter leaves, salty prosciutto and crunchy almonds.

Ingredients

8 ripe figs, sliced

4 heirloom tomatoes, sliced

12 slices prosciutto

5 oz/150 g endive leaves, picked

1 cup/8 oz/250 g fresh ricotta cheese

½ teaspoon sea salt flakes

½ teaspoon cracked black pepper

½ cup/2 oz/60 g whole roast almonds, roughly chopped

2 tablespoons lemon juice

1¼ fl oz/40 ml extra virgin olive oil

1 tablespoon maple syrup

1 teaspoon seeded mustard

1 tablespoon sweet balsamic glaze

Baby basil leaves, to garnish

Method

Arrange the figs, tomatoes, prosciutto and endive onto the base of serving plates or a large serving platter.

Mix together the ricotta, salt and pepper until well combined then crumble over the salad.

Whisk together the lemon juice, olive oil, maple syrup and mustard in a small bowl and drizzle over the top. Season the salad with an extra pinch of sea salt and finish with a small drizzle of the balsamic glaze over the top. Scatter with almonds, baby basil leaves and serve.

Note

Balsamic glaze is available at selected supermarkets and specialty food stores.

NYC Waldorf Salad with Candied walnuts & Blue Cheese

Serves 4 as a light meal

Many versions of the classic combination of apple, walnuts and celery have been created over the years. My version is inspired by one I ordered at the Standard Hotel in NYC. This version has a light creamy dressing, smoky bacon, wafer thin slices of apple for texture and mild blue cheese for a bit of bite.

Ingredients

For the Candied Walnuts:

2 tablespoons caster (superfine) sugar

12 fresh whole walnuts

2 rashers (strips) smoked bacon, cut into lardons

2 cups/4 oz/115 g frissee lettuce, washed

2 cups/4 oz/115 g cos lettuce, baby or inner leaves, washed

1 stalk celery, finely diced

1 Granny Smith apple, washed and finely sliced

2 oz/60 g mild blue cheese, crumbled

Baby mustard cress, to garnish

For the Dressing:

2 fl oz/60 ml buttermilk

1 tablespoon quality mayonnaise

Pinch white pepper

1 tablespoon lemon juice

1 teaspoon honey

Method

Place the sugar and ¼ cup/2 fl oz/60 ml water in a small pan. Place over a medium-high heat and stir to dissolve the sugar. Bring to the boil and cook for 5–7 minutes, or until the mixture turns a golden colour.

Add the walnuts, stir to coat all the nuts with the caramel, then pour onto a lined tray and spread the nuts out to cool and set. Break into pieces. Set aside.

Meanwhile, cook the bacon in a small frying pan set over a medium heat until crisp. Place onto kitchen paper to remove any excess fat. Set aside.

Whisk all the dressing ingredients together in a bowl.

To serve, place the frissee, cos lettuce, celery, apple and blue cheese onto a serving plate. Scatter over the bacon and walnuts. Drizzle with the dressing and garnish with the mustard cress.

Beef

Beef & Brown Rice Korean Salad Bowl

Serves 4

This dish provides a little bit of everything all in one bowl! You can substitute any of your favourite vegetables into the mix and, of course, vegetarians can swap the beef for grilled tofu.

Ingredients

1 cup/7 oz/200 g brown rice, washed
500 g/1lb 2 oz beef fillet, finely sliced
1 tablespoon ginger, grated
2 garlic cloves, grated
1 tablespoon brown sugar
2 tablespoons soy sauce
2 teaspoons sesame oil
¼ cup/2 fl oz/60ml sunflower oil
1 large carrot, sliced into ribbons
2 green zucchini (courgettes), sliced into ribbons
1 bunch English spinach, washed and trimmed
4 free-range eggs
2 green spring onions (scallions), finely sliced
2 teaspoons sesame seeds, toasted
½ cup/4 fl oz/125 ml gochujang chilli dressing (see page 19)

Method

Cook the brown rice according to packet instructions, set aside and keep warm.

Coat the beef with the ginger, garlic, brown sugar, soy sauce and sesame oil in a non-metallic container.

Heat ¾ fl oz/20 ml of the sunflower oil over a medium/high heat in a large non-stick frying pan. Cook the beef in batches for 2–3 minutes, or until just cooked through. Remove the beef and set aside in a bowl.

Heat a little more oil in the same pan over a medium heat and add the carrot and zucchini. Cook for 2 minutes, then add in the English spinach and continue to cook for another 2 minutes, or until the spinach has wilted. Return the beef to the pan to warm through for 2 minutes.

Heat the remaining oil in a non-stick frying pan and fry the eggs for 2–3 minutes, or until just set.

To serve divide the brown rice between the serving bowls. Top the rice with the beef and vegetables, then place the fried egg over the top and drizzle with the gochujang chilli sauce, spring onions and scatter over sesame seeds.

Beef & Buckwheat Noodle Salad with Wafu Dressing

Serves 4

For the last four years, I've been catering for a professional football team and I make this dish for them all the time. It's full of protein, it's healthy and after all, all it takes is a little red meat to persuade boys to eat salad!

Ingredients

2 tablespoons soy sauce

2 tablespoons mirin

1 tablespoon caster (superfine) sugar

9½ oz/270 g dried buckwheat soba noodles

1 lb 2 oz/500 g whole beef fillet

2 tablespoons olive oil

2 garlic cloves, sliced

5 oz/150 g beanshoots

5 oz/150 g enoki mushrooms

2 small Lebanese cucumbers, sliced into ribbons

2 green shallots, finely sliced

1 cup Wafu dressing (see page 29)

1 teaspoon Japanese seven spice mix*

Method

Preheat the oven to 180°C/350°F/Gas mark 4.

Whisk together the soy sauce, mirin and sugar in a large bowl. Add the beef fillet and leave to marinate at room temperature for 45 minutes.

Heat half of the olive oil in a non-stick frying pan. Remove the beef from the marinade and put into the pan and fry for 2 minutes on each side, or until seared. Place the beef onto an oven tray and roast for 15 minutes for rare, or longer if desired. Remove the beef from the oven and allow to rest for 10 minutes before slicing.

Meanwhile, cook the noodles in a pan of boiling salted water for 3 minutes. Drain and refresh under cold water and set aside.

Heat the remaining oil in a large non-stick fry pan over a high heat. Add the garlic, beanshoots and enoki mishrooms. Cook, tossing for 1–2 minutes, or until the garlic is fragrant. Remove from the heat and set aside.

To serve, place the noodles onto a serving platter along with the cucumber, green shallots, beanshoot mixture and sliced beef. Drizzle over the wafu dressing and sprinkle with the seven spice mix.

Notes

*Japanese seven spice mix is available from Asian supermarkets. Substitute fried shallots, chilli flakes, peanuts or sesame seeds for the spice mix, if you prefer.

Vitello Tonnato with Eggs & Capers

Serves 4

This classic Italian dish has been around for years. I have cut out a few steps for a quicker, more modern take on this wonderful combination of veal and tuna!

Ingredients

1 lb 6oz/600 g veal fillet, trimmed of all sinews and sliced into 4 logs lengthways
Sea salt flakes
2 tablespoons olive oil
¼ bunch/2 tablespoons thyme sprigs
4 eggs
1 small lemon, to serve
1 cup/5 oz/150 g baby rocket (arugula), picked
Cracked black pepper, to garnish
Micro parsley, to garnish

For the Tuna Sauce:

6 oz/185 g best quality tinned tuna in oil, drained
2 anchovy fillets, chopped
4 boiled eggs, chopped
1 tablespoon baby capers, washed, plus extra to serve
2 tablespoons lemon juice
2 teaspoons lemon zest
100 ml/3½ fl oz olive oil

Method

Heat a non-stick frying pan over a medium heat.

Season the veal pieces with sea salt and rub over the oil before placing into the frying pan along with the thyme sprigs. Cook the veal, turning after 2–3 minutes on each side, or until cooked through. Remove from the heat, discard the thyme and set aside to rest in a warm place.

Meanwhile, cook the eggs in boiling salted water for 6–8 minutes, refresh under cold water, peel, slice in half and set aside.

For the tuna sauce, place the tuna, anchovies, eggs, capers, lemon juice, zest and a pinch of sea salt and pepper into a food processor. Blend until mostly combined then slowly pour in the oil and blend for 30–40 seconds, or until you have a smooth dressing that is slightly thinner than mayonnaise.

To serve, slice the veal into thin rounds and arrange on a serving platter. Add a generous dollop of tuna sauce and garnish with eggs, rocket leaves, extra capers, micro parsley, cracked black pepper, lemon and a drizzle of olive oil.

Lemongrass Beef with Noodle & Herb Salad

Serves 4

This herby noodle salad can be made with any protein. I've used beef here but it'd work just as well with chicken, lamb, pork, shrimp or tofu. Feel free to experiment!

Ingredients

1 lb 2 oz/500 g piece beef eye fillet, trimmed and sliced

1 tablespoon vegetable oil

2 tablespoons Asian-fried shallots

2 tablespoons Kewpie Japanese mayonnaise

1 teaspoon sriracha chilli sauce

1 tablespoon black sesame seeds

For the Marinade:

2 tablespoons lemongrass, finely chopped (white part only)

1 tablespoon fresh root ginger finely chopped

1 tablespoon coriander (cilantro) stems, finely chopped

2 garlic cloves, crushed

1 tablespoon fish sauce (nam pla)

1 tablespoon honey

½ teaspoon black pepper

1 teaspoon sesame oil

For the Noodle Salad:

7 oz/200 g rice vermicelli noodles

2 cups/4 oz/115 g iceberg lettuce, finely sliced

1 long red chilli, sliced

2 green shallots, finely sliced

1 medium carrot, peeled and cut into julienne strips

1 cup/2½ oz/80 g coriander (cilantro), torn

1 cup/2½ oz/80 g mint, torn

For the Dressing:

1 tablespoon white vinegar

1 tablespoon white (granulated) sugar

1 teaspoon fish sauce (nam pla)

1 teaspoon chilli oil (or fresh chilli)

½ teaspoon sesame oil

White pepper

Lime juice, to taste

Method

Place the sliced beef in a large bowl, cover with all the marinade ingredients and leave to marinate for 1 hour.

Place the noodles in a large bowl and cover with boiling water and leave to stand for 5 minutes. Cut the noodles a few times with scissors, drain and rinse to cool.

Place the cooled noodles in a large bowl and add in all the salad ingredients.

Mix all the dressing ingredients together in a bowl. Set aside.

Combine the mayonnaise and siracha in a small bowl. Set aside.

Heat the oil in a large non-stick frying pan over a high heat. Cook the beef in batches for 3–4 minutes, or until cooked to your liking. Remove the beef from the heat and set aside in a warm area.

To serve, place the noodle salad onto a serving platter, top with the cooked beef. Drizzle with the dressing, sriracha mayonnaise and scatter over the fried shallots and black sesame. Garnish with extra coriander and a wedge of lime.

Bresaola with Celeriac, Apple & Watercress

Serves 4

This lovely, light salad is best served as an entrée or a starter. Bresaola (originally from Italy) is air-dried salted beef that has been aged for 2–3 months until it becomes hard and the colour is transformed to a deep red tone.

Ingredients

1 small celeriac, peeled and
    sliced into fine julienne strips
1 Granny Smith apple, sliced
    into fine julienne strips
2 tablespoons quality
    mayonnaise
1 tablespoon Greek (strained
    plain) yogurt
1 tablespoon lemon juice,
    plus extra to serve
2 teaspoons honey
20 slices bresaola
1 bunch watercress, leaves
    picked and washed
2 green spring onions
    (scallions), finely sliced
1 tablespoon extra virgin
    olive oil
Sea salt flakes

Method

Place the celeriac and apple into a large bowl.

Combine the mayonnaise, yogurt, lemon, honey and a pinch of sea salt together in a small bowl. Mix through the apple and celeriac until well combined. Arrange the sliced bresaola onto serving plates and top with a mound of the celeriac salad and watercress leaves. Sprinkle with sliced spring onion and drizzle with oil.

Naked Beef Burger with Mushroom, Cheese & Pickle

Serves 4

This is the ultimate amateur dish—it's so easy to make! I prefer to fill-up on salads and vegetables rather than heavy carbs all the time so I've simply replaced the burger bun for lettuce cups. Think of this as a type of san-choy-burger!

Ingredients

4 iceberg lettuce outer leaves, washed and trimmed
1 lb 2 oz/500 g Angus (ground) beef mince
1 teaspoon fresh thyme, finely chopped
1 teaspoon fresh rosemary, finely chopped
1 tablespoons olive oil
1 large brown onion, finely sliced
2 large field (Portobello) mushrooms, sliced
4 slices tasty (Cheddar) cheese
1 large tomato, sliced
8 slices canned beetroot, drained
4 dill pickles, sliced lengthways
¼ cup/2 fl oz/60 ml American mustard
½ cup/4 fl oz/125 ml tomato chutney
1 teaspoon dried chilli flakes, optional
Sea salt flakes and pepper

Method

Put the beef in a bowl and add the thyme, rosemary and a generous pinch of salt and pepper. Using clean hands, mix the herbs through the mince. Divide the mixture into four even portions and form into patties about ½ in/1 cm thick.

Heat a large non-stick frying pan over a medium heat. Add the oil to the pan and when hot, add the beef patties. Cook for 2 minutes, then add the mushrooms and onions to the same pan along with a pinch of salt. Turn the burgers over and cook for another 2–3 minutes on the second side, or until cooked through. Remove the beef patties from the pan, top with the cheese and set aside to rest.

Continue to cook the mushrooms and onions for 2 minutes, or until soft. Remove from the heat.

To serve, place the lettuce leaves on a serving board. Place the tomato and beetroot in the centre of the leaves. Top with the mushroom and onion mixture. Squeeze over the tomato chutney and mustard. Place on the beef patties and scatter over the dill pickles and chilli, if using. Serve immediately.

Beef Carpaccio with Tomato, Basil & Pecorino

Serves 4

Beef served in a salad like this is melt-in-the-mouth soft. Sweet roast tomatoes, salty olives and fresh herbs are my favourite topping, but feel free to change the flavour combinations, if you wish.

Ingredients

7 oz/200 g beef fillet

7 oz/200 g cherry tomatoes, quartered

2 fl oz/60 ml extra virgin olive oil

1 teaspoon caster (superfine) sugar

½ cup/1¼ oz/40 g basil leaves, finely sliced

3 oz/90 g pecorino cheese, peeled with a vegetable peeler

20 small black olives, pits removed

20 sorrel leaves

1 tablespoon balsamic glaze

Sea salt flakes and pepepr

Method

Heat 20 ml of olive oil in a large non-stick frying pan set over a medium-high heat. Season the beef fillet with sea salt flakes and seal in the pan for 2–3 minutes, turning, so all of the outside of the beef fillet is golden. Remove from the pan and wrap the beef tightly in plastic wrap (cling film) and freeze for 1 hour, or until firm but not frozen through.

Meanwhile, heat the oven to 160°C/325°F/Gas mark 3.

Put the tomatoes onto a lined oven tray and drizzle with half of the olive oil, all the sugar and season with sea salt flakes. Bake for 30-35 minutes, or until the tomatoes have slightly dried and become wrinkly and sweet. Remove and allow to cool.

Remove the beef from the freezer and unwrap. Using a very sharp knife, cut the beef across the grain into paper thin slices. Arrange the beef onto serving plates slightly overlapping and season with sea salt and pepper. Top the beef with the roast tomatoes, basil, pecorino cheese, olives and sorrel leaves. Drizzle with the remaining olive oil and balsamic glaze.

Meatball Salad

Serves 4 (Makes 12 Large Meatballs)

It might seem strange to have meatballs in a salad but once you've tried this, you won't think it's so strange... It's amazeballs in fact! In winter, ribbons of warm vegetables work well as a base for the meatballs. Here's to filling-up on all the good stuff!

Ingredients
For the Meatballs:
1 lb 2 oz/500 g (ground) pork mince

1 lb 2 oz/500 g (ground) beef mince

1 free-range egg, lightly beaten

⅔ cup/5½ oz/165 g fresh ricotta cheese

2 oz/60 g Parmesan, finely grated

2 teaspoons thyme, finely chopped

2 teaspoons rosemary, finely chopped

1 tablespoon tomato paste

For the Tomato Sauce:
1 tablespoon olive oil

1 small brown onion, diced

2 garlic cloves, crushed

¼ cup/2 oz/60 g tomato paste

3 x 14 oz/400 g can crushed tomatoes

½ teaspoon dried chilli flakes, plus extra to serve (optional)

2 teaspoons sugar

2 teaspoons dried oregano

⅔ cup/2½ oz/75 g frozen peas

7 oz/200 g rocket (arugula), washed

20 black olives, pits removed

½ cup/1 ¼ oz/40 g basil leaves, picked

1 tablespoon balsamic glaze

Sourdough bread, to serve

Method
Pre-heat the oven to 180°C/350°F/Gas mark 4.

Mix together all the meatball ingredients in a large bowl until well combined. Roll into 12 large meatballs, place into a deep-sided large oven tray and set aside in the refrigerator.

For the tomato sauce, heat the oil over a medium heat in a saucepan. Cook the onion and garlic for 3–4 minutes, or until softened. Add in the tomato paste, crushed tomatoes, chilli, sugar and oregano. Bring the sauce to a gentle simmer and cook, stirring occasionally for 5–6 minutes.

Remove the meatballs from the refrigerator and pour the tomato sauce over the top of the meatballs in the tray. Place into the oven and cook for 40–45 minutes, occasionally gently rolling the meatballs around to ensure they are covered in sauce and the tops of the meatballs don't dry out. Remove from the oven and allow to rest for 10 minutes before serving.

Meanwhile, blanch the peas in a pan of salted, boiling water for 2–3 minutes. Drain and refresh the peas under cold water to cool.

To serve, divide the rocket, peas and olives onto the base of serving bowls. Place the meatballs on top of the salad and scatter over the basil leaves, balsamic glaze and a little extra grated Parmesan. Serve warm with sourdough bread.

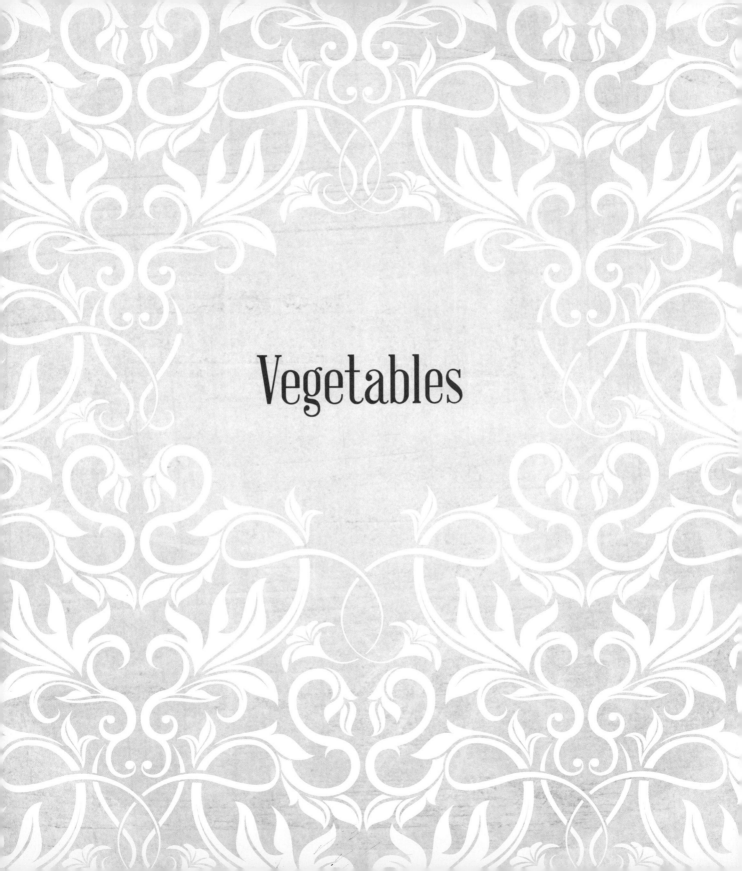

Vegetables

Green Quinoa with Pesto & Toasted Seeds

Serves 4

I used to have a health-based cooking segment on one of the morning TV shows. I was always coming up with new healthy salads that were quick and easy (to fit into the limited time allocated), but still wanted them to be interesting to the viewer. It was a good indication if the recipes were any good or not if the hosts asked for them to be put aside for their lunch. This recipe was whisked away as soon as the segment was over! Weeks later, the hosts told me they loved it so much, they'd cooked it a few times since... It's pretty good for you too!

Ingredients

1¾ oz/50 g red quinoa seeds

1¾ oz/50 g while quinoa seeds

6 oz/180 g broccolini, trimmed

1 cup/4 oz/115 g frozen peas

5 oz/150 g baby spinach leaves

½ cup/4 fl oz/125ml fresh basil pesto (see page 25)

1 avocado, peeled and sliced

1¾ oz/50 g pepita seeds, toasted

1¾ oz/50 g sunflower seeds, toasted

3½ oz/100 g feta cheese, crumbled

Lemon wedges, to serve

Method

Place the quinoa seeds into a pan and cover with 400 ml/14 fl oz of cold water. Bring to the boil, then reduce the heat to a low a simmer and cook for 12–14 minutes, or until the quinoa is fluffy and all the liquid has been absorbed.

Meanwhile, blanch the broccolini in salted boiling water for 2 minutes, before adding in the peas and cooking for a further 2 minutes. Drain and place the greens into a large bowl with the cooked quinoa.

Add the spinach and pesto to the bowl and toss well to combine.

Place the quinoa salad onto serving plates or bowls then scatter over the avocado, pepita and sunflower seeds, feta and a squeeze of lemon juice.

Note

This salad is great on its own, but will go well with grilled (broiled) fish or roast chicken.

Spicy Kale, Edamame &
Pickled Ginger Salad

Serves 4

Edamame beans and pickled ginger are two of my favourite Japanese ingredients. It's the type of salad I make for a quick and healthy lunch at home. The ponzu will keep for 2 weeks in the refrigerator, so having it on hand will make it easy to whip up tasty treats for lunch.

Ingredients

7 oz/200 g frozen podded
   Edamame beans (soybeans)
1 tablespoon olive oil
4 large brown (Portobello)
   mushrooms, sliced
1 garlic clove, peeled and
   sliced
8 kale leaves, stalks removed,
   finely sliced
1 ripe avocado, peeled and
   sliced
2 green shallots, finely sliced
1¾ oz/50 g pickled ginger
2 tablespoons Kewpie
   mayonnaise*
2 teaspoons nanami togarashi
   (Japanese assorted chilli
   pepper)

For the Ponzu Dressing:

½ ckove garlic, finely grated
1 tablespoon yuzu*
1 tablespoon tamari soy sauce
1 tablespoon mirin
1 tablespoon rice wine vinegar
1 tablespoon brown sugar
1 teaspoon sesame oil
Ground white pepper

Method

Cook the edamame beans in a pan of boiling salted water for 4–5 minutes, drain then refresh under cold water to cool and set aside.

Heat the olive oil in a non-stick frying pan set over a medium heat. Add the mushrooms and cook for 2–3 minutes. Add the garlic and a pinch of sea salt and continue to cook for another 2–3 minutes then set aside to cool.

Whisk together all the dressing ingredients in a large bowl and add the edamame beans, mushrooms, kale, avocado and green shallots. Toss well to dress then place into a serving bowl. Top the salad with the pickled ginger, kewpie mayonnaise and sprinkle with the nanami togarashi chilli powder.

Notes
Edamame soybeans, yuzu and nanami toarashi are available from Asian supermarkets.
*Kewpie mayonnaise and mirin are available from the Asian section of the supermarket.

Raw Rainbow Beetroot & Apple Salad with Feta & Toasted Seeds

Serves 4

I love throwing a raw salad into the mix every now and then! You get all the nutritional value out of the vegetables. The beetroot adds a great, earthy flavour and if you can find different coloured varieties to create a visually interesting salad, even better!

Ingredients

4 medium sized beetroots, different colours, peeled and cut into thin matchsticks

40 ml olive oil

20 ml lemon juice

20 ml maple syrup

1 teaspoon whole cumin seeds

¼ cup/1½ oz/45 g sunflower seeds

¼ cup/1½ oz/45 g pepita seeds

2 red apples, skin on, cut into thin matchsticks

5 oz/150 g feta

1 cup/2½ oz/80 g fresh mint leaves, picked

Sea salt and freshly ground black pepper

Method

Place the beetroot into a large bowl. Mix together half of the oil, lemon juice and maple syrup and season with a generous pinch of sea salt and black pepper. Pour the dressing over the raw beetroot, mix well and set aside.

Heat a small pan over a medium heat and add the cumin seeds, sunflower and pepita seeds. Toast the seeds with remaining of oil for 3–4 minutes, or until golden and crunchy. Remove from the heat and allow to cool.

Mix the apple through the beetroot along with half the mint and place onto a serving platter. Add the feta cheese, remaining mint leaves and scatter with toasted seeds and any remaining juices.

Asian Pickled Vegetable & Sesame Salad

Serves 4–6

Pickling vegetables before adding them to a salad is a great way of creating interesting flavours and textures.

Ingredients

2 medium zucchinis (courgettes), sliced into matchsticks

2 teaspoons sea salt

2 cups Chinese cabbage (wombok), finely sliced

1 long red chilli, seeds removed and finely sliced

1 cup/2½ oz/80 g Thai basil, picked

1 cup/2½ oz/80 g fresh mint leaves, torn

1 cup/2½ oz/80 g fresh coriander (cilantro), roughly chopped

2 green shallots, finely sliced

1 tablespoon sesame seeds, toasted

For the Pickle Mix:

⅔ cup/5½ fl oz/165 ml white vinegar

½ cup/3½ oz/100 g white (granulated) sugar

¼ cup/2 fl oz/60 ml water

For the Dressing:

⅓ cup/2½ fl oz/75ml Pickle Mix

2 teaspoons soy sauce

2–3 drops chilli oil

2 teaspoons sesame oil

White pepper

Method

For the pickle mix, place the vinegar, sugar and water in a small pan and set over medium heat. Stir for a few minutes, until the sugar has dissolved. Simmer gently for 5 minutes, or until the mixture becomes slightly syrupy. Leave to cool.

Place the zucchini and carrots in a bowl and sprinkle over the salt. Gently rub the salt into the vegetables with clean hands, and leave for 15 minutes. Drain through a sieve (this will get rid of all the salt as well as the excess liquid).

Tip the zucchini and carrot into a glass bowl and cover with the pickle mix. Leave for 15 minutes to 'pickle'.

Meanwhile, place the cabbage, chilli, Thai basil, mint, coriander, shallots and sesame seeds, in a large bowl.

Drain the zucchini and carrot (reserving one-third of a cup of the liquid for the dressing) Place the pickled vegetables in with the remaining salad.

Mix all the dressing ingredients in a bowl, and pour over the salad. Toss the salad lightly to coat evenly with dressing, and place onto a serving platter.

Scatter over extra coriander leaves.

Watercress, White Peach, Bocconcini & Almond Salad

Serves 4 as part of a banquet

Like most extremely simple salads, this one really is all about the quality of the produce you use. White peaches are sweetly delicious, but only have a short season. Find the best peaches you can for this salad. It will be worth the little bit extra you spend! I like to use white peaches in as many dishes as I can whilst they are good. They pair perfectly with the peppery rocket leaves and milky cheese in this super simple salad.

Ingredients

2 cups watercress leaves,
    picked and washed
1 teaspoon oil
2 teaspoons honey
2 cups/10 oz/280 g baby rocket
    (arugula) leaves, washed
2 large ripe white peaches,
    washed and halved
4 large bocconcini cheese,
    roughly torn
¼ cup/1 oz/30 g flaked
    almonds, toasted
¼ cup/2 tablespoons micro red
    sisho leaves, cut

For the Dressing:

2 tablespoons white wine
    vinegar
2 teaspoons honey
2 tablespoons olive oil
Sea salt flakes and white pepper

Method

Heat the oil in a non-stick frying pan set over a medium heat. Place the peaches in the pan skin side down and fry for 2–3 minutes, or until caramelised. Turn the peaches over and drizzle with the honey. Cook for another 1–2 minutes to warm the honey, before removing the peaches from the heat.

To serve, arrange the watercress, rocket, peaches and bocconcini on a serving platter. Mix all the dressing ingredients together, pour over the salad. Top with the toasted almonds and sisho leaves. Serve immediately.

Tamari & Agave Roast Pumpkin with Nuts & Seeds

Serves 4 as a side dish

I absolutely love sweet, roasted pumpkin. It can be used in a variety of cuisines. This recipe is great as a side dish to accompany other elements such as roast chicken, barbecued fish and leafy, green salads.

Ingredients

2½ lb/1 kg Jap pumpkin, seeded and sliced into ¾ in/2 cm thick wedges
¼ cup/2 fl oz/60ml olive oil
40 ml tamari soy sauce
2 tablespoons agave syrup, plus extra to serve
¼ cup/1 oz/30 g unsalted cashews, roughly chopped
¼ cup/2 tablespoons Asian fried golden shallots
1 tablespoon toasted sesame seeds
Sea salt flakes and ground white pepper

Method

Preheat the oven to 180°C/350°F/Gas mark 4.

Place the pumpkin in a bowl and toss with the oil. Lightly season with sea salt and ground white pepper then arrange on a lined oven tray and roast for 35 minutes. Remove from the oven and drizzle with the tamari and agave. Return to the oven and cook for another 10–15 minutes, or until the pumpkin is cooked through and golden. Remove from the oven and arrange on a serving platter. Drizzle with extra agave syrup, if desired, then top with the cashews, fried shallots and sesame seeds. Serve warm.

Roast Heirloom Carrots with Yogurt & Za'atar

Serves 2 as a side dish

If you can find different coloured heirloom carrots, great! If you can't, don't worry because regular carrots sliced lengthways and roasted will work just as well in this recipe.

Ingredients

8 heirloom carrots, washed and halved
½ fl oz/20 ml olive oil
1 teaspoon sea salt flakes
1 teaspoon whole cumin seeds
1 tablespoon honey
½ cup/4 fl oz/125 ml tahini yogurt (see page 16)
1 tablespoon za'atar (see page 21)

Method

Preheat the oven to 180°C/350°F/Gas mark 4.

Coat the carrots with olive oil, salt and cumin then place onto a lined oven tray. Roast for 20–25 minutes, or until the carrots are golden and cooked through.

Remove from the oven and while the carrots are still hot drizzle over the honey and toss to coat. Arrange the carrots onto a serving plate and add a dollop of tahini yogurt and sprinkle with za'atar.

Steamed Eggplant Salad with Ginger & Black Vinegar Dressing

Serves 4 as part of a banquet

I have a weakness for eggplant. If it's ever on the menu, I'll always order it! Steaming eggplant, gives it a lovely, custard-like texture. This eggplant recipe is my favourite thing to serve as part of an Asian banquet.

Ingredients

2 medium eggplant (aubergine), top removed and sliced lengthways into 8 wedges

2 teaspoons sea salt

2¾ fl oz/80 ml peanut oil

¼ cup/2 tablespoons fresh root ginger, sliced into julienne strips

2 teaspoons caster (superfine) or brown sugar

1 teaspoon sesame oil

1 tablespoon tamari soy sauce

2 teaspoons chinkiang Chinese black vinegar

¼ cup green shallots, sliced

¼ cup coriander (cilantro), sliced

Method

Sprinkle both sides of the eggplant with salt. Place in a single layer on a tray. Set aside for 10 minutes. (This removes any bitterness from the eggplant.)

Meanwhile, to make the dressing, place the peanut oil in a pan set over a high heat, and bring to smoking point. Place the ginger into a heatproof bowl then carefully pour the hot oil over the ginger. Once it has stopped bubbling, add the sugar, sesame oil, soy sauce and black vinegar. Stir to combine and check for balance. Set aside.

Put the eggplant in a colander and rinse well. Drain and pat dry with kitchen paper.

Arrange the eggplant onto a heatproof plate and fit inside a steamer basket. Place over a deep saucepan of boiling water and steam, covered, for 15–20 minutes, or until the eggplant is just tender.

Carefully remove eggplant from steamer and allow to cool slightly.

To serve, arrange eggplant onto a serving platter and spoon over the dressing. Sprinkle with spring onions and coriander sprigs.

Agrodolce Zucchini Salad

Serves 4

This quick and easy salad is great served with whole grilled fish, roast chicken or try it as a sandwich filler.

Ingredients

¾ oz/20 g pine nuts
¾ oz/20 g slivered almonds
2 tablespoons sherry vinegar
1½ tablespoons caster (superfine) sugar
½ garlic clove, finely chopped
2 tablespoons olive oil
2 large zucchini (courgettes), sliced into julienne strips
½ red onion, finely sliced
1 oz/30 g currants
½ cup/40 g/1 ¼ oz flat leaf parsley, chopped
Sea salt flakes and black pepper

Method

Dry roast the nuts in a small frying pan set over medium heat until golden, 2–3 minutes. Set aside.

Put the vinegar and sugar in a small pan and bring to a simmer over a medium-high heat, stirring until the sugar dissolves. Add the garlic and season to taste. Remove from heat and leave to cool for 5 minutes, then whisk in the oil.

Combine the zucchini and onion in a large bowl. Pour over the dressing, toss to combine and leave to stand for 10–15 minutes to infuse. Toss through the pine nuts, almonds, currants and parsley before serving.

Almond, Cranberry & Herb Quinoa Salad

Serves 6–8

This salad is all about texture. A healthy mix of nutty quinoa, earthy seeds, crunchy nuts and as always, a citrusy dressing to tie it all together. I have cooked this at many of my dinner parties and I am constantly asked for the recipe... So here it is...

Ingredients

1 cup/6 oz/175 g white quinoa seed
1 cup/6 oz/175 g pearl couscous
¼ cup/1½ oz/45 g sesame seeds, toasted
½ cup/2 oz/60 g walnuts, chopped
½ cup/2 oz/60 g slivered almonds, toasted
¼ cup/1½ oz/45 g pepita seeds
¼ cup/1½ oz/45 g sunflower seeds
¼ cup/2 oz/60 g currants
¼ cup/1½ oz/45 g dried cranberries
½ cup/1 ¼ oz/40 g flat leaf parsley, chopped
½ cup/1 ¼ oz/40 g mint, chopped
½ cup/1 ¼ oz/40 g coriander (cilantro), chopped

For the Dressing:

⅓ cup/2½ fl oz/75 ml olive oil
Sea salt flakes and pepper
2 tablespoons honey
⅓ cup/2½ fl oz/75 ml lemon juice

Method

Place the quinoa in a pan, cover with 2 cups of cold water and set over a medium heat. Bring up to the boil, then turn down to a gentle simmer and cook for 12-14 minutes, or until all the liquid has been absorbed and the quinoa is fluffy. Set aside to cool. Place the pearl couscous in a pan of cold water, and set over medium heat. Bring to a simmer and cook for 12 minutes. Drain and leave to cool.

Place all the dressing ingredients in a small bowl, whisk and set aside.

In a large bowl, place the quinoa, pearl couscous, sesame seeds, walnuts, almonds, pepita seeds, sunflower seeds, currants, cranberries, parsley, mint and coriander. Mix well, and pour over the dressing, and toss to coat.

Place the salad into a serving bowl and garnish with extra mint and coriander.

Heirloom Tomato, Buffalo Mozzarella with Mixed Herb Pesto

Serves 4

Heirloom tomatoes are a little more expensive than the regular varieties, but this salad is so simple that the quality of the tomatoes, mozzarella and olive oil is extremely important. The different coloured tomatoes have varying amounts of sweetness and texture, so choose your favourites and pay a little extra for the ingredients and they will speak for themselves!

Ingredients

1 cup/8 fl oz/250 ml herb and almond pesto (see page 26)
600 g/1 lb 6 oz Heirloom tomatoes, mixed sizes and colours
2 large fresh buffalo mozzarella balls (or 12 cherry bocconcini balls, drained)
1 teaspoon sea salt flakes
2 tablespoons olive oil
Greek baby basil leaves to garnish, picked

Method

Put half of the pesto in the centre of a large serving platter.

Cut the tomatoes into slices, quarters and halves. Arrange the tomatoes on top of the pesto. Season with the sea salt.

Roughly tear the mozzarella cheese and place around the tomatoes. Spoon over the remaining pesto, then drizzle with olive oil and scatter over the Greek basil leaves.

Spiced Cauliflower Salad with Mustard Yogurt

Serves 4

I love roasted vegetable salads, particularly in winter when you're looking for something a little more homely. This roast cauliflower salad is great served as a side dish or you could add some grilled chicken or roast lamb with a handful of salad leaves to enjoy as a meal.

Ingredients

1 head cauliflower, outer greens removed and cut into florets
2 tablespoons olive oil
2 teaspoons whole cumin seeds
1 teaspoon ground coriander
½ teaspoon ground cinnamon
2 tablespoons slivered almonds, toasted
1 tablespoon dried currants

For the Mustard Yogurt:

1 cup/8 fl oz/250 ml thick Greek (strained plain) yogurt
2 teaspoons Dijon mustard
1 tablespoon lemon juice
2 teaspoons honey

Method

Preheat the oven to 180°C/350°F/Gas mark 4.

Place the cauliflower, in a large bowl and toss with the oil, cumin seeds, coriander and cinnamon and season with sea salt.

Place the cauliflower onto a lined oven tray and roast for 25–30 minutes, or until golden and fragrant.

Meanwhile, mix all the yogurt dressing ingredients together in a bowl until well combined. Place the yogurt dressing on the base of a serving platter. Top with cauliflower and sprinkle over the almonds and currants. Serve warm.

Warm Brussels, Roast Garlic
& Black Tahini Dressing

Serves 2

Roasting Brussels sprouts gives them a more intense flavour and texture, compared to just boiling them. If you're not usually a sprout lover, just give these a try!

Ingredients

6 garlic cloves, skin left on
14 medium Brussels sprouts,
  trimmed and halved
2 tablespoons olive oil
1¼ oz/40 g labneh cheese (see
  page 22)
¼ cup/2 tablespoons flat leaf
  parsley, sliced
Sea salt flakes

For the Dressing:

2 teaspoons black tahini
1 tablespoon apple cider
  vinegar
1 tablespoon honey
1 tablespoon olive oil

Method

Preheat the oven to 180°C/350°F/Gas mark 4.

Place the garlic in the middle of a piece of foil and drizzle with 1 tablespoon of oil and a pinch of sea salt. Seal the foil into a pouch, place on a baking tray and roast for 30–35 minutes.

Meanwhile, bring a pan of salted water to the boil and blanch the Brussels sprouts for 3–4 minutes. Drain, then drizzle the Brussels with the remaining oil and a pinch of sea salt.

Place the Brussels sprouts onto a lined oven tray and place in the oven with the garlic and roast for 15–20 minutes, or until golden. Leave to cool slightly.

Mix all the dressing ingredients together, season and whisk until well combined.

To serve, place the Brussels sprouts and roast garlic onto a warm serving plate. Break over the labneh cheese, drizzle with tahini dressing and garnish with parsley. Serve warm.

Note

Black tahini can be found in specialty food stores. Tahini is ground sesame seeds that form a loose paste. Black tahini is made with black sesame seeds.

Crunchy Quinoa Salad with Pear, Celery, Cashews & Parmesan

Serves 4

I've called this 'crunchy quinoa salad' because it's just that! You get a lovely mix of textures from the crunchy celery, crispy pear, creamy cashews and nutty quinoa seeds.

Ingredients

2¾ oz/80 g white quinoa seeds

2 green pears, washed

2 celery stalks, washed and finely sliced

3 cups/6 oz/175 g Cos lettuce leaves, washed and finely sliced

½ cup/40 g/1 ¼ oz flat leaf parsley, chopped

3½ oz/100 g Parmesan, shaved

½ cup/2 oz/60 g roasted cashews

2 fl oz/60 ml extra virgin olive oil

2 tablespoons lemon juice

1 tablespoon honey

1 tablespoon seeded mustard

Method

Place the quinoa in a pot, cover with 320 ml/11 fl oz of cold water and place onto a medium heat. Bring to the boil, turn down to a gentle simmer and cook for 12–14 minutes, or until the quinoa is fluffy and all the liquid has absorbed.

Cut the pears into quarters, remove the core and using a mandolin or sharp knife, shave the pear into very thin wedges.

Place the quinoa, pear, celery, lettuce, parsley, Parmesan and cashews into a large bowl.

Whisk together the oil, lemon, honey, mustard and a good pinch of sea salt and pepper. Pour the dressing over the salad and toss well to coat. Divide the salad into bowls and serve.

Blood Orange, Roast Beetroot & Hazelnut Salad

Serves 4

This is a really simple recipe to make. It looks spectacular with all the different colours. If blood oranges are not in season, substitute them for regular oranges, which will work just as well.

Ingredients

2 bunches (12 small) baby beetroot, washed, trimmed, small leaves reserved
1 bunch (4 medium) golden beetroot, washed and trimmed
2 fl oz/60 ml olive oil
½ cup/1¼ oz/40 g thyme leaves
4 blood oranges, peeled and sliced
⅓ cup/1½ oz/40 g roasted hazelnuts, roughly chopped
6 oz/180 g marinated goat's cheese, drained and crumbled
Red micro cress, to garnish
Baby Greek basil, to garnish

For the Dressing:

40 ml olive oil
1 tablespoon Chardonnay vinegar
2 teaspoons maple syrup
Sea salt flakes and pepper

Method

Preheat the oven to 180°C/350°F/Gas mark 4.

Coat the beetroot in the oil and season with a generous pinch of sea salt. Wrap the beetroot and thyme in foil packages and place them onto an oven tray. Roast the beetroot for 35–40 minutes, or until tender when a sharp knife is inserted into the centre. Remove from the oven and allow to rest in the foil for 15 minutes. Remove the skin and slice into quarters.

Arrange the sliced blood orange rounds on the base of a large serving platter. Scatter over the roast beetroot, hazelnuts, goat's cheese, reserved baby beetroot leaves, red cress and Greek basil. Drizzle over the dressing and serve.

Notes
Golden beetroots are from selected supermarkets and farmers' markets.
Micro herbs are from selected supermarkets and gourmet fruit shops. You can replace the micro herbs with any of your favourite soft herbs.

Broad Bean, Pea, Lemon
& Goat's Cheese

Serves 2

A flavourful spring dish; if fresh peas are available, then use them instead of frozen. Same goes for the broad beans.

Ingredients

1 cup/5 oz/175 g fresh broad (fava) beans, podded

1½ cups/6 oz/150 g frozen peas

2 oz/60 g goat's cheese

2 teaspoons lemon zest, finely sliced

1 teaspoon red chilli, finely sliced

Cracked black pepper, to serve

For the Dressing:

1 tablespoon lemon juice

1 tablespoon olive oil

1 teaspoon honey

½ teaspoon sea salt flakes

Method

Bring a pan of salted water to the boil and add the beans. Cook for 3–4 minutes, then remove the beans with a slotted spoon and transfer to a plate.

Once cool enough to handle, peel the outer skin from the beans and discard. Set aside.

Place the same pan back onto the heat and bring it back up to a boil. Add the peas and cook for 2–3 minutes, or until just cooked. Drain and place them into a shallow serving dish along with the beans.

Scatter over the goat's cheese, lemon zest and chilli.

Mix all the dressing ingredients together and pour over the salad. Top with cracked black pepper and serve.

Snake Bean, Tofu &
Sesame Quinoa Salad

Serves 4

This is a delicious protein-packed vegetarian/vegan salad. It is fantastic eaten, but also keeps very well for a few days when refrigerated. It is perfect leftovers for a healthy desk lunch or picnic dish!

Ingredients

1 tablespoon sunflower oil
300 g/10½ oz snake beans, or green beans, trimmed, sliced into ⅛ in/0.5 cm rounds
3½ oz/100 g five-spiced tofu, diced
2 teaspoons ginger, grated
2 garlic cloves, grated
½ teaspoon five-spice powder
3½ oz/100 g white quinoa seeds, cooked according to the packet instructions
¼ cup/1½ oz/45 g sesame seeds, toasted
2 green shallots, finely sliced

For the Dressing:

2 tablespoons light soy sauce
2 tablespoons sunflower oil
2 tablespoons rice wine vinegar
1 tablespoon brown sugar
2 teaspoons sesame oil
1 teaspoon chilli oil
¼ teaspoon ground white pepper

Method

Mix all the dressing ingredients together in a bowl and set aside.

Heat the oil in a large non-stick fry pan set over a medium/high heat. Add the snake beans and cook, stirring for 3–4 minutes before adding the tofu, ginger, garlic, five-spice powder and a small pinch of sea salt. Continue to cook for another 2–3 minutes, or until the beans are cooked and the tofu has warmed through.

Place the beans into a large bowl along with the cooked quinoa, sesame seeds and green shallots. Pour over the dressing and toss together. Place the salad onto a serving dish and eat while still warm.

Beetroot Salad with Spiced Almonds & Goat's Cheese

Serves 4

This flavour combination has been around for a while...And the main reason is it works! Earthy roasted beetroot goes perfectly with any creamy soft cheese. I've used goats cheese in this recipe, but also feta, ricotta and fresh mozzarella would work. The almonds can also be replaced with hazelnuts, pine nuts, cashews, pistachios or toasted seeds such as sunflower or pepitas.

Ingredients

2 bunches (12 small) baby beetroot, golden and regular

1 fl oz/30 ml olive oil

4 sprigs thyme

1 cup/5 oz/150 g baby rocket (arugula) leaves

7 oz/200 g soft goat's cheese

1 cup/4 oz/115 g spiced maple almonds (see page 31)

For the Dressing

1 fl oz/30 ml red wine vinegar

1 tablespoon maple syrup

1½ fl oz/40 ml extra virgin olive oil

1 teaspoon Dijon mustard

Sea salt flakes and pepper

Method

Preheat the oven to 180°C/350°F/Gas mark 4.

Wash and trim the leaves from beetroot, reserving the smaller ones for the salad. Place four 12 in/30 cm lengths of foil on a bench and divide the beetroot between the foil and place in the centre. Drizzle the olive oil over the beetroot, scatter with thyme leaves and season with sea salt. Seal the foil tightly around the beetroot, place on an oven tray and bake for 30–40 minutes, or until the beetroots are cooked through. Remove from the oven and allow to cool before peeling off the skin and slicing in half.

Whisk all the dressing ingredients together in a bowl and season with a pinch of salt and pepper.

Arrange the rocket, baby beetroot leaves and cooked beetroot on a serving platter. Crumble over the goat's cheese and drizzle with the dressing. Scatter with almonds and serve.

Note
Golden beetroot is available from selected greengrocers and farmers' markets.

Crispy Cos Salad with Roast Corn & Creamy Dressing

Serves 4

Roasting or grilling corn gives it a smoky flavour created when the natural sugars in the corn caramelize. Smoky sweet corn is a great way to add depth of flavour to a simple salad such as this one!

Ingredients

3 cobs corn, husks removed

1 tablespoon olive oil

4 cups/8 oz/250 g Cos lettuce, washed and sliced

1 small fennel bulb, finely sliced and fronds reserved

4 red radishes, washed and finely sliced

½ cup/4 fl oz/125 ml salad cream dressing (see page 20)

Sea salt flakes

Method

Heat a non-stick fry pan over a medium heat.

Coat the corn with the olive oil, season with sea salt flakes and cook for 10–12 minutes, turning occasionally until the corn is charred on the outside and cooked through. Remove from the heat and allow the corn to cool before slicing off the kernels.

In a large bowl, combine the lettuce, fennel, radish, corn and salad cream dressing. Toss well to coat everything in the dressing and place into serving bowls. Scatter over the fennel fronds.

Japanese-Style Roast Pumpkin & Quinoa Salad

Serves 4

This is a great salad for sharing, or one to make if you have a crowd to entertain. Of course it's hearty enough to eat on its own, or perfect when served alongside roast meats or grilled seafood!

Ingredients

800 g/1 ¾ lb Jap pumpkin, skin on, seeded, cut into 3/8 in/1 cm thick wedges

2 tablespoons olive oil

1 teaspoon dried chilli flakes

1 cup/6 oz/175 g white quinoa seeds, rinsed

7 oz/200 g frozen podded edamame beans (soybeans)

4 small radishes, finely sliced

3½ oz/100 g baby rocket (arugula) leaves, washed

¼ cup/1 ¼ oz/40 g pepita seeds, toasted

1 tablespoon sesame seeds, toasted

Baby sisho leaves, to garnish

For the Ponzu Dressing:

1 tablespoon yuzu

1 tablespoon tamari soy sauce

1 tablespoon mirin

1 tablespoon rice wine vinegar

1 tablespoon brown sugar

1 teaspoon sesame oil

Ground white pepper

Method

Preheat the oven to 180°C/350°F/Gas mark 4.

Place the pumpkin onto a lined oven tray, drizzle with the olive oil and sprinkle with dried chilli and a generous pinch of sea salt flakes. Place the pumpkin in the oven and roast for 30–35 minutes, or until the pumpkin is tender, but still holding its shape. Remove from the oven and allow to cool.

Meanwhile place the quinoa into a pot and cover with 2 cup/17 fl oz/500 ml of cold water. Place onto a medium heat and bring up to the boil, turn down to a gentle simmer, cover and cook for 12–14 minutes or until the quinoa is fluffy and all the liquid has been absorbed.

Cook the edamame beans in a pan of salted boiling water for 2–3 minutes, then drain and refresh under cold water.

Whisk all the dressing ingredients together in a bowl and set aside.

To serve, place the quinoa on the base of a serving platter. Layer the pumpkin, radish, rocket and edamame beans on top of the quinoa. Drizzle over the dressing and garnish with pepita seeds, sesame seeds and baby sisho leaves.

Notes
Edamame, yuzu and mirin are available from Asian supermarkets.
Tamari soy is a wheat-free soy sauce available form selected supermarkets and health food stores.

Smashed Chickpea & Quinoa Tabouleh with Pomegranate

Serves 4

Traditional tabouleh is made with cracked wheat. I have exchanged the wheat for quinoa and smashed chickpeas in the dish, not just for dietary reasons, making it gluten and wheat free... but because it gives a variety of textures and most of all tastes delicious!

Ingredients

2¾ oz/80 g white quinoa seeds, rinsed

1 x 14 oz/400 g can chickpeas, drained and rinsed

1 cup/2½ oz/80 g flat leaf parsley, finely chopped

½ cup/1 ¼ oz/40 g mint leaves, finely chopped

¼ cup/2 tablespoons chives, finely sliced

2 large ripe tomatoes, seeded and diced

1 small pomegranate, seeds removed

1 ¾ fl oz/50 ml extra virgin olive oil

40 ml lemon juice

1 tablespoon honey

1 teaspoon sea salt

2 tablespoons pomegranate molasses

Method

Place the quinoa into a pan and cover with 320 ml/11 fl oz of cold water. Place onto a medium-high heat and bring to the boil, then turn down to a gentle simmer. Cover and cook for 12–14 minutes, or until the quinoa is fluffy and all the water has absorbed. Set aside.

Place the chickpeas into a large bowl and using the back of a fork, roughly smash half of the chickpeas leaving some whole for texture. Add in the parsley, mint, chives, tomato, cooked quinoa and half the pomegranate seeds.

Whisk together the olive oil, lemon juice, honey and salt. Pour over the salad and toss well to coat.

Place the salad onto a serving platter and top with the remaining pomegranate seeds and drizzle with pomegranate molasses.

Raw Squash Salad

Serves 4

Squash simply dressed with some olive oil, Parmesan cand fresh herbs are divine. Easy peasy too!

Ingredients

6 large yellow squash, washed
2 large green zucchini
(courgettes), washed
4 red radishes, washed
¼ cup/2 tablespoons fresh
mint, leaves picked
¼ cup/2 tablespoons fresh
basil, leaves torn
2 ¾ oz/80 g Parmesan, freshly
grated
¼ cup/1 oz/30 g roasted
almonds, roughly chopped
40 ml olive oil
Sea salt flakes and ground
black pepper

Method

Using a mandolin, slice the squash, zucchini and radishes into thin round discs.

Arrange the vegetables into a large serving platter. Scatter over the mint, basil, Parmesan and almonds. Drizzle with the olive oil and a pinch of sea salt flakes and cracked black pepper.

Deep-Fried Brussels Sprouts, Crispy Chickpeas & Spiced Yogurt

Serves 4

It seems a bit naughty to deep fry a perfectly good vegetable, and it probably is, but sometimes all that matters is if it tastes good or not! I will let you be the judge here. Very addictive though.

Ingredients

3½ pints/2 litres sunflower oil
1 lb 2 oz/500 g Brussels
   sprouts, halved lengthways
1 x 14 oz/400g can chickpeas,
   drained
1 teaspoon paprika
1 cup/8 fl oz/250 ml Greek
   (strained plain) yogurt
1 tablespoon tahini paste
1 teaspoon dried chilli flakes
2 teaspoons cumin powder
2 teaspoons honey
¾ fl oz/20 ml lemon juice
¾ fl oz/20 ml olive oil
¼ cup/2 tablespoons fresh
   mint, finely sliced
1 tablespoon sesame seeds,
   toasted

Method

Heat 1 litre of the oil in a large heavy pan and the remaining 1 litre in a smaller heavy pan. Bring both pans to 170°C/340°F.

Dry the chickpeas very well on kitchen paper. Place them into a bowl and toss with the paprika and carefully place them into the smaller pan of oil and cook for 6–8 minutes, or until crispy. Remove from the oil, drain on paper towel and season with sea salt. Set aside.

Meanwhile, fry the Brussels sprouts for 10–12 minutes, or until the outer leaves are golden and crisp in the larger pan. Remove from the oil and drain on kitchen towel.

Combine the yogurt, tahini, dried chilli, cumin, honey, lemon and olive oil in a bowl.

Place the spiced yogurt on the base of a large serving bowl. Place the Brussels on top of the yogurt and scatter over the chickpeas, mint and sesame seeds.

Seed & Nut Raw Beetroot Slaw

Serves 4

A mandolin is perfect for cutting all the vegetables in this recipe quickly and evenly. If you don't have a mandolin you can use a toothed vegetable peeler or just cut everything as finely as you can with a sharp knife.

Ingredients

4½ oz/120 g baby spinach leaves, roughly chopped

2 medium beetroot, peeled, sliced into matchsticks

2 medium green zucchini (courgettes), sliced into matchsticks

2 long red chillies, seeds removed, sliced into strips

½ cup/3 oz/85 g pomegranate seeds

⅓ cup/1½ oz/40 g slivered almonds, toasted

⅓ cup/2 oz/60 g sunflower seeds, toasted

⅓ cup/2 oz/60 g pepita seeds, toasted

⅓ cup/1½ oz/40 g unsalted roasted cashew nuts

1 tablespoon white sesame seeds, toasted

For the Dressing:

2 fl oz/60 ml extra virgin olive oil

1 fl oz/30 ml sherry vinegar

1 tablespoon honey or maple syrup

1 teaspoon sea salt flakes

Pinch ground white pepper

Method

Whisk all the dressing ingredients together in a large bowl. Add all the remaining ingredients except the beetroot. Toss well to coat everything in the dressing.

Add the beetroot and gently toss once or twice before placing the salad into serving bowls.

Serve on its own or with your favourite cheese, grilled (broiled) meats, poultry or fish.

Spiced Falafel &
Beetroot Slaw Salad

Serves 4 and makes around 20 falafel

Using dried chickpeas gives a wonderful texture and bite to the falafel, so please don't be tempted to use canned chickpeas, as they are too soft for this recipe. I really love this eaten as a salad, but it could also work wrapped in warm flat bread as a sort-of kebab.

Ingredients
For the Falafel:
9 oz/250 g dried chickpeas
2 tablespoons cumin seeds
2 tablespoons coriander seeds
2 teaspoons ground all spice
½ teaspoon ground chilli
2 teaspoons baking powder
1 onion, finely chopped
3 cloves garlic, crushed
1 cup/2½ oz/80 g flat leaf
    parsley, chopped
1 cup/2½ oz/80 g coriander
    (cilantro), chopped
2 teaspoons sea salt
½ teaspoon ground white
    pepper
1 tablespoon plain (all-
    purpose) flour
¼ cup/1½ oz/45 g white
    sesame seeds
14 fl oz/400 ml sunflower oil,
    for frying

For the Beetroot Slaw:
2 large raw beetroot, peeled, finely sliced into matchsticks
5 oz/150 g red cabbage, cored, finely sliced
½ red onion, finely sliced
2 tablespoons quality mayonnaise
2 tablespoons Greek (strained plain) yogurt, plus extra to serve

¼ cup/2 tablespoons mint leaves, torn
Lemon wedges, to serve

Method
Start this recipe the night before.

Place the dried chickpeas into a bowl, cover with cold water and leave to soak overnight.

The next day, drain the chickpeas and discard the water.

Toast the cumin and coriander seeds in a small frying pan set over a medium heat for 1 minute, or until fragrant. Remove from the heat and crush the seeds into a fine powder using a mortar and pestle or coffee grinder.

Place the ground spices into a food processor along with all the other falafel ingredients, except the sesame seeds. Blitz until everything has combined to make a rough paste. Form the mixture into tablespoon-size balls. Coat with sesame seeds and set aside on a tray in the refrigerator for 30 minutes for the flavours to develop.

Meanwhile, combine all the beetroot slaw ingredients together in a bowl, season with a pinch of salt, mix well and set aside.

Heat the oil to 160°C/320°F in a saucepan or deep fryer. Make sure the oil is not too hot as the falafel will cook too quickly and not cook through. If the oil is too cool, the falafel will become oil logged. Cook the falafel, in batches for 3–4 minutes or until golden and fragrant. Drain on kitchen towel.

To serve, place the beetroot slaw onto the base of the serving bowls. Top with the warm falafel and drizzle with extra yogurt, scatter over mint leaves and serve with lemon wedges.

Crisp Tofu Salad with Spicy Peanut Dressing

Serves 4

This is my version of the classic Indonesian gado gado. Some versions include boiled potato, chopped tomatoes and chunks of cucumber. I have omitted them from this recipe, but feel free to add in any of these as well to the mix. Grilled shrimp or poached chicken make a great addition to this salad too.

Ingredients

4 free-range eggs

5 oz/150 g marinated pressed tofu, cut into strips

2 garlic cloves, peeled and sliced

1 cup/8 fl oz/250ml sunflower oil, for frying

9 oz/ 250 g snake beans, trimmed

7 oz/200 g Chinese cabbage (wombok), finely sliced

3½ oz/100 g bean sprouts

Sea salt flakes and black pepper

For the Spicy Peanut Dressing:

2 tablespoons sunflower oil

½ red onion, diced

1 tablespoon ginger, finely sliced

2 garlic cloves, sliced

1 long red chilli, chopped, plus extra to serve

1 tablespoon tamarind paste

1 tablespoon brown sugar

1 cup/4 oz/115 g roasted plain peanuts

7 fl oz/200 ml coconut milk

Method

To make the dressing, heat the oil in a small saucepan over a medium heat and add the onion and ginger. Cook, stirring for 3–4 minutes, then add the garlic and chilli and continue to cook for another 2–3 minutes, or until fragrant and soft.

Add the tamarind, sugar, peanuts and ¼ cup/2 fl oz/60 ml water. Simmer for 2–3 minutes, then remove from the heat and allow to cool slightly before blending in to a smooth past in the bowl of a food processor. Place the paste into a saucepan set over a medium heat. Pour in the coconut milk and simmer, stirring for 8–10 minutes, or until the oil starts to split form the sauce. Check for seasoning and keep warm.

Cook the eggs in a pot of salted boiling water for 6–8 minutes. Remove the eggs from the heat and place them into a bowl of chilled water. Once cool enough to handle peel the eggs and set aside.

Heat the oil in a wok or deep fryer to 160°C/325°F. Dry the tofu with paper towel and fry for 1–2 minutes, or until golden. Remove with a slotted spoon and drain on kitchen towel. Fry the garlic for 1–2 minutes, or until golden and crisp. Remove from the oil and drain on kitchen towel.

Heat 1 tablespoon of the oil used to fry the tofu over a high heat in a large frying pan. Cook the snake beans for 3–4 minutes. Remove from the heat and set aside to cool slightly.

To serve, place the Chinese cabbage and bean shoots onto a large serving platter. Add the snake beans and tofu and break over the eggs. Spoon over the peanut dressing and garnish with the fried garlic and extra chopped red chilli.

Note
Snake beans, tamarind and marinated pressed tofu are from Asian supermarkets or specialty green grocers.

Garam Masala Roast Pumpkin with Yogurt & Seeds

Serves 4

Ingredients

1¾ lb/800 g Jap pumpkin, skin on, sliced into wedges

2 fl oz/60 ml olive oil

2 teaspoons ground garam masala

1 teaspoon sea salt flakes

2 teaspoons white sesame seeds

1 teaspoon poppy seeds

1 teaspoon ground cumin

7 oz/200 g mixed salad leaves

1 x 14 oz/400 g can lentils, drained and rinsed

For the Yogurt Dressing:

1 cup/8 fl oz/250 ml thick Greek (strained plain) yogurt

1 tablespoon tahini paste

1 tablespoon lemon juice

2 teaspoons honey

Pinch sea salt

Method

Preheat the oven to 180°C/350°F/Gas mark 4.

Coat the pumpkin in the olive oil, garam masala and sea salt. Place onto a lined oven tray and roast for 30–35 minutes, or until the pumpkin is tender, but still holding its shape. Remove from the oven and set aside to cool slightly.

Heat a small non-stick frying pan over a medium heat and toast the sesame seeds and poppy seeds for 2–3 minutes, or until fragrant and golden. Remove from the heat and stir the ground cumin through the seeds while they are still hot.

Whisk all the yogurt dressing ingredients together in a bowl until smooth.

To serve, place the salad leaves and lentils onto the base of serving bowls. Arrange the roast pumpkin over the top of the leaves and drizzle with the yogurt and scatter over the seeds.

Brussels Sprout Slaw with Miso, Edamame & Shaved Egg

I make this salad all the time. It is great on its own for a light meal or it will go perfectly with fresh sashimi, grilled fish, tofu, chicken or beef for a more substantial meal.

Ingredients

4 free-range eggs

7 oz/200 g frozen podded edamame, skins removed

1 lb 2 oz/500 g Brussels sprouts, finely shaved

1 tablespoon black sesame seeds

For the Miso Dressing:

2 tablespoons white miso paste (shiro)

2 tablespoons rice wine vinegar

1 tablespoon mirin

1 tablespoon caster (superfine) sugar

1 tablespoon light soy sauce

1 tablespoon olive oil

1 teaspoon sesame oil

Method

Cook the eggs in a pan of salted boiling water for 10–12 minutes. Remove from the heat and place into a bowl of chilled water to cool completely. Peel and set aside in the refrigerator.

Meanwhile, cook the edamame in a pan of salted boiling water for 2–3 minutes. Refresh under running cold water, drain and set aside.

In a bowl, whisk together all the dressing ingredients along with 1 tablespoon of warm water until smooth.

Place the edamame beans and shaved Brussels sprouts into a large bowl. Pour over the dressing and toss well to coat, then place into serving bowls.

Using a medium sized grater, grate the boiled eggs over the top of each salad. Scatter over the sesame seeds and serve.

Notes

Edamame are Japanese green soybeans.

Mirin is a Japanese cooking wine. Both are available from Asian food shops.

Beetroot, Edamame &
Qunioa Salad with Ponzu

Serves 4

My Ponzu dressing is used on a few different salads throughout this book, because I just love the citrusy, sweet, salty combination. It's not just for Japanese style dishes. Try it out on all different types of salads.

Ingredients

4 medium beetroot, trimmed, washed
2 fl oz/60 ml olive oil
2¾ oz/80 g red quinoa seeds
5 oz/150 g frozen podded edamame beans (soybeans)
2 bunches/400 g/14 oz broccolini, trimmed
5 oz/150 g baby spinach or mixed leaves
1 teaspoon black sesame seeds
2 blood oranges, peeled, sliced into rounds
½ cup/1 ¼ oz/40 g coriander (cilantro), leaves picked
1 teaspoon chilli oil
Sea salt flakes

For the Ponzu Dressing:

1 tablespoon yuzu
1 tablespoon tamari soy sauce
1 tablespoon rice wine vinegar
1 tablespoon mirin
1 tablespoon brown sugar
1 teaspoon sesame oil
White pepper

Method

Preheat the oven to 180°C/350°F/Gas mark 4.

Place each beetroot onto an 8 in/20 cm length of foil. Drizzle the beetroot with half of the oil and season with a pinch of sea salt. Seal the foil around the beetroot and place in an oven tray. Roast for 40 minutes, or until tender. Remove from the oven and allow to cool before slipping the skins off the beetroot and cutting into rounds. Set aside.

Meanwhile, place the quinoa into a pan and cover with 320ml /11 fl oz of cold water. Place onto a high heat and bring to the boil before reducing the heat to a gentle simmer. Cook the quinoa for 12-14 minutes, or until it is fluffy and all the liquid has been absorbed. Set aside to cool.

Cook the edamame beans in a large pan of salted boiling water for 2 minutes, add the broccolini and continue to cook for another 2–3 minutes. Drain and refresh under cold water. Slice the broccolini in half lengthways, set aside.

Whisk all the ponzu ingredients together in a bowl until the sugar has dissolved.

To serve, place the baby spinach, quinoa, edamame, broccolini and sesame seeds in a large bowl. Pour over the dressing and toss well. Divide the salad into serving bowls and place over the beetroot, blood orange, coriander and chilli oil.

Note
Edamame beans, yuzu and mirin are available at Asian supermarkets.

Carrot Salad, Carrot Top Pesto, Quinoa & Cumin Yogurt

Serves 2

This is a wonderful, tasty salad to make in the cooler months. Roasted carrots are deliciously sweet and make a great addition to all kinds of salads. The combination of nutty quinoa, spiced yogurt and herby pesto makes for a lovely Autumn brunch or lunch.

Ingredients

1 bunch Dutch baby carrots, leafy tops washed and reserved
¾ fl oz/20 ml olive oil
1 ¾ oz/50 g red quinoa seeds, rinsed
2 cups/10 oz/280 g baby rocket (arugula) leaves
1¾ oz/50 g goat's cheese
¼ cup/1 oz/30 g pistachio nuts, chopped

For the Carrot Top Pesto:

½ cup /4 tablespoons green leafy carrot tops, plus extra to garnish
¼ cup/2 tablespoons coriander (cilantro), leaves picked
¼ cup/2 tablespoons mint, leaves picked
¼ cup/1 oz/30 g unsalted roasted cashews

1 tablespoon lemon juice
2 teaspoons honey
¾ oz/20 g Parmesan, grated
2½ fl oz/80 ml olive oil
Sea salt flakes

For the Cumin Yogurt:

1 teaspoon whole cumin seeds
½ cup/4 fl oz/125 ml Greek (strained plain) yogurt
1 tablespoon quality mayonnaise

Method

Preheat the oven to 180°C/350°F/Gas mark 4.

Coat the carrots in the olive oil and season with a pinch of sea salt. Place them on a lined oven tray and roast for 25–30 minutes, or until tender and cooked through.

Meanwhile, place the quinoa in a pot, cover with 7 fl oz/200 ml of cold water and place onto a medium-high heat. Bring up to the boil, turn heat down to a gentle simmer, cover and cook for 12–14 minutes, or until the quinoa is fluffy and all the liquid has absorbed. Set aside.

Place all the carrot top pesto ingredients into a small food processor, blend until smooth and set aside.

Heat a small frying pan over a medium heat, add the cumin seeds and toast for 30 seconds, or until fragrant. Remove the seeds from the heat and grind to a fine powder in a mortar and pestle or coffee grinder. Mix the ground cumin, a pinch of sea salt flakes, yogurt and mayonnaise together in a bowl until combined.

Spoon the yogurt dressing onto the base of serving plates and top with the quinoa, rocket leaves and carrots. Scatter over the goat's cheese, pesto, pistachio nuts and reserved extra carrot tops.

Chilli Slaw with Beanshoots, Dill & Cashew Nuts

Serves 4

Here is a super easy, no-cook crisp mix of bean sprouts, shaved cabbage, creamy cashews and crunchy apple. I like to serve this salad with BBQ ribs, chicken or grilled fish.

Ingredients

3½ oz/100 g fresh bean sprouts

7 oz/200 g savoy cabbage, finely sliced

3½ oz/100 g red cabbage, finely sliced

1 carrot, peeled and sliced into julienne strips

3½ oz/100 g broccoli stalks, trimmed and cut into thin matchsticks

1 green apple, sliced into thin matchsticks

2 green spring onions (scallions), finely sliced

¼ cup/2 tablespoons fresh dill, chopped

⅔ cup/2½ oz/75 g roasted cashews

1 long red chilli, seeds removed and finely sliced

For the Dressing

2 tablespoons Kewpie mayonnaise

2 teaspoons sriracha chilli sauce

2 teaspoons rice wine vinegar

2 teaspoons sesame oil

2 teaspoons fish sauce (nam pla)

2 teaspoons brown sugar

Method

Whisk all of the dressing ingredients together in a bowl until smooth.

Place all of the slaw ingredients into a large bowl and pour over the dressing and mix well. Divide the slaw between the serving bowls.

Notes

Kewpie mayonnaise is a Japanese mayonnaise available from selected supermarkets and Asian food stores.

Sriracha chilli sauce is a hot chilli paste available from Asian supermarkets.

Indian Spiced Cauliflower 'Couscous'

Serves 4

A great recipe for those that can't or don't eat grains, rice or potatoes! Blitzing the cauliflower and gently steaming it is a tasty, gluten-free, vegan and low carb alternative to regular couscous or rice.

Ingredients

2¼ lb/1 kg whole cauliflower

2 tablespoons olive oil

1 large red onion, finely sliced

1 tablespoon ginger, finely chopped

1 teaspoon brown mustard seeds

½ cup/1½ oz/40 g coriander (cilantro), washed

1 garlic clove, crushed

1 teaspoon ground coriander

1 teaspoon ground cumin

1 teaspoon ground turmeric

1 long red chilli, seeded, finely chopped

1½ oz/40 g butter

1 teaspoon sugar

¾ fl oz/20 ml lemon juice

½ teaspoon garam masala

¾ cup/3 oz/85 g cashews, toasted

Sea salt flakes

Method

Cut the thickest stems off the cauliflower and reserve for stock or soup. Trim the florets into small chunks and place in batches into a food processor and pulse until they look like couscous. Don't over-blend or it will become mushy.

Heat the oil in a large non-stick frying pan set over a medium heat. Cook the onion with a pinch of sea salt for 6–8 minutes, or until golden. Add the ginger and mustard seeds and cook for another 2 minutes.

Finely chop the stems of the coriander and add to the pan, reserving the leaves for garnish. Add in the garlic, ground coriander, cumin, turmeric and chilli. Continue to cook for another 1–2 minutes to toast the spices.

Add the butter to the pan and once melted, add the cauliflower and a pinch of sea salt and stir well to coat everything in the spices. Place a lid on the pan and cook, covered, for 2–3 minutes, or until the cauliflower is tender, but still holding its shape. Remove from the heat and stir through the sugar, lemon juice and garam masala. Place onto a serving platter and sprinkle with the cashews and coriander leaves.

Grilled Corn, Blackbean &
Smoked Almond Salad

Serves 4 as part of a banquet

This is a great smoky flavoured salsa type salad. It can be served on its own as a salad, or as part of a Mexican feast with slow-cooked pulled meats, warm tortillas and creamy guacamole. Ole.

Ingredients
4 fresh corn cobs, peeled
1 tablespoon olive oil
Sea salt flakes and pepper
1 large avocado, diced
10½ oz/285 g jar roasted
   capsicum, drained and
   roughly chopped
1 can black/turtle beans
   drained
½ bunch/1½ oz/40 g coriander
   (cilantro), roughly chopped
½ bunch/1½ oz/40 g mint,
   roughly chopped
⅔ cup whole smoked almonds,
   roughly chopped

For the Dressing:
Juice of 2 limes
1 tablespoon agave syrup
2 tablespoons olive oil

Method
Place the corn into a large non-stick fry pan along with a pinch of salt and brush with the olive oil. Grill the corn for 8–10 minutes, turning occasionally until slightly blackened on the outside. Remove the corn from the heat, allow to cool slightly. Cut the kernels from the cob and place in a large bowl. Add the diced avocado, roast capsicum, black beans, coriander and mint.

Combine all the dressing ingredients together in a bowl and pour over the salad. Toss to combine. Place the salad onto a serving plate and scatter over the smoked almonds. Enjoy.

Miso-Glazed Eggplant Salad

Serves 4

This dish is really easy to make and has few ingredients to prepare. Serve these creamy savoury delights with any type of grilled meat, seafood or tofu. A bowl of lightly dressed greens will also sit nicely alongside them.

Ingredients

6 medium eggplant (aubergines)
2 teaspoons sea salt
2 fl oz/60 ml olive oil, for brushing
3½ oz/100 g white shiro miso paste*
1¾ oz/50 g caster (superfine) sugar
40 ml mirin
40 ml sake
2 teaspoons white sesame seeds, toasted
1 tablespoon chives, finely sliced

Method

Preheat the oven to 180°C/350°F/Gas mark 4.

Slice the eggplants in half lengthways and cut a few shallow slits in the flesh of on the diagonal. Sprinkle with the sea salt and leave for 15 minutes for some of the bitterness and moisture to be drawn out. Rinse the salt off and pat dry with kitchen towel.

Brush the eggplant with the oil and fry in a non-stick frying pan set over a medium heat for a few minutes on each side until golden, but not cooked all the way through. Transfer the eggplants flesh side up onto a lined oven tray.

Whisk together the miso, sugar, mirin and sake until a smooth paste. Brush the miso glaze over the eggplants, then bake the eggplants in the oven for 10–12 minutes, or until tender and the miso glaze is bubbling and fragrant. Remove from the oven and arrange onto a serving platter. Sprinkle over the sesame seeds and chives. Serve warm.

Note: Miso paste and mirin are from selected supermarkets and Asian food stores.

Crumbed Eggplant Salad with Harissa Yogurt & Dukkah

Serves 4

It takes a little bit of time to prepare this salad, but it's well worth it. Crumbing and frying the eggplant gives it a fantastic crispy coating outside, with a silky texture inside. However, feel free to oven bake, or grill the eggplants for a slightly healthier version.

Ingredients

2 eggplant (aubergine) (10½ oz/300 g each), sliced into 3/8 in/1 cm thick rounds
1 cup/4 oz/115 g plain (all-purpose) flour
2 teaspoons turmeric
1 tablespoon garam masala
1 free-range egg
½ cup/4 fl oz/125 ml milk
2 cups/6 oz/150 g breadcrumbs
2 cups/16 fl oz/500 ml sunflower oil
1 x 14 oz/400g can chickpeas, drained
3½ oz/100 g baby rocket (arugula) leaves
¼ cup dukkah (see page 30)
Small fresh coriander (cilantro) leaves, to serve
Sea salt flakes and pepper

For the Harissa Yogurt:

1 cup/8 fl oz/250 ml Greek (strained plain) yogurt
2 teaspoons harissa paste
1 tablespoon lemon juice
2 teaspoons honey

Method

Place the eggplant onto a lined tray in a single layer. Sprinkle with 2 teaspoons of sea salt flakes and leave for 15–20 minutes for the salt to draw some of the bitterness out of the eggplant and to remove some of the moisture. Rinse the salt off and pat the eggplant dry with kitchen towel.

Combine the flour, turmeric and garam masala in a large bowl. Season with sea salt and pepper and coat the eggplant in the flour mixture.

In a separate large bowl, whisk the egg and milk together. Dip the eggplant into the egg mixture and drain off any excess liquid before coating the eggplant in the breadcrumbs.

Heat the oil in a large frying pan set over a medium heat. Cook the eggplant, in batches for 2–3 minutes each side, or until golden on the outside and creamy in the middle. Drain on kitchen towel to remove any excess oil.

Meanwhile, combine all the harissa yogurt ingredients together in a bowl.

To serve, line a large platter with a layer of the crumbed eggplant. Top with the chickpeas and rocket. Drizzle over the yogurt dressing and garnish with dukkah and baby coriander leaves.

Index

ACKNOWLEDGEMENTS

MY FELLOW SALAD LOVERS – This book is for you, enjoy!

MUM & DAD – For passing on your enthusiasm for food and thrifty ability to create a meal from barely any ingredients! You've taught me to be resourceful and the memories of meals we ate growing up still stay with me today. Thank you also for forcing me to eat Brussels sprouts and oysters when I refused as a child. I have grown to love all types of food because of this!

DIANE & THE NEW HOLLAND TEAM – Never in my wildest dreams did I think I would have my own cookbook! This opportunity and support you have given has helped bring my dreams to life. Thank you.

SUE STUBBS – The wonderful photographer I had the pleasure of working alongside during the shoot of this book. Thanks for sharing your personal music selection with me and relieving me of my huge abundance of 'salady' leftovers!

EMMA DUCKWORTH – My very own personal food stylist! Thanks for making my food look clean, pretty and most of all, utterly delicious!

CARMEL HORVATH AND COLES SUPERMARKETS – For your continual friendship and support over the years, and supplying all the delicious ingredients for this book.

THE SYDNEY SWANS- For the use of your kitchen facilities & a venue for my shoots! Without that huge fridge, I would have been lost!

And... last but certainly not least…

MY PARTNER IN CRIME SOPHIE – My fiancé, my best friend and my favorite food critic! Your constant support and motivation makes anything possible. Thank you for your loving and caring nature and your patience with my technological handicap! I am forever grateful to have you by my side.

First published in 2015 by New Holland Publishers Pty Ltd
London • Sydney • Auckland

The Chandlery Unit 009 50 Westminster Bridge Road London SE1 7QY United Kingdom
1/66 Gibbes Street Chatswood NSW 2067 Australia
5/39 Woodside Ave Northcote, Auckland 0627 New Zealand

www.newhollandpublishers.com

A record of this book is held at the British Library and the National Library of Australia.

ISBN 9781742576244

Managing Director: Fiona Schultz
Publisher: Diane Ward
Project Editor: Angela Sutherland
Designer: Lorena Susak
Typesetter: Peter Guo
Production Director: Olga Dementiev
Printer: Toppan Leefung Printing Limited

10 9 8 7 6 5 4 3 2 1

Keep up with New Holland Publishers on Facebook
www.facebook.com/NewHollandPublishers